*LIVE FOR TOMORROW*

# LIVE FOR TOMORROW

## By Ralph W. Sockman

⟫ ✳ ⟪

1939 · THE MACMILLAN COMPANY · NEW YORK

107729

241.45
So 13

PRINTED IN THE UNITED STATES OF AMERICA
BY THE VAIL-BALLOU PRESS, INC., BINGHAMTON, N. Y.

*Dedicated to*
*The Congregation*
*of the*
*National Radio Pulpit*

# FOREWORD

THIS book goes to press on the day that Hitler goes into Poland. Why write about living for tomorrow when men are killing one another today? Foolish indeed seems he who would venture to outline a future as fluid as the map of Europe. But this book attempts nothing so ambitious as a diagram of tomorrow's world. It is only a design for personal living in that world.

A popular vogue of writing during the last few years has been to withdraw from the brutal and baffling world scene into the comfortable precincts of personal psychology and encouragement. To be sure, the mind is its own place and can make a heaven for itself even while hell is being let loose in a new war. Pleasant it is to read nice little books on the art of brightening the corner where you are. But if such comfortable reading satisfies us in a time like this, there is something wrong with ourselves. In these pages we have not sought to close the blinds on dark realities but rather to open the windows to catch whatever light we can.

Some of the material was given as the Henry Martin Loud lectures at the University of Michigan under the auspices of the First Methodist Church of Ann Arbor. Deep gratitude is expressed to Dr. Charles W. Brashares, the minister of that church, and to the others who made the author's stay so pleasant. One or two of the chapters formed part of a lecture series before the Pastors' Conference at Western Maryland College and sincere appreciation is given to President Fred G. Holloway and the Reverend Earl Cummings for their many courtesies accorded the speaker. To Mrs. Helen V. Putnam, Miss Sara H. Alexander and Mr. Francis Purcell, thanks are due for assistance in the preparation of the manuscript. To Miss Harriet C. Woodworth the author is indebted for valuable research.

# CONTENTS

*LIVE FOR TOMORROW*

# Chapter 1

# A TRUCE WITH TIME

SHORTLY after the United States entered the Great War, Lord Balfour of England and Henri Bergson, the distinguished philosopher of France, were together in New York City. They had come to arouse American interest in the cause of the Allies. After speaking at a great mass meeting they retired to the home of Joseph H. Choate. There, while the city was seething with war excitement, these two eminent representatives of their respective governments talked long into the night. About what? The military crisis? No. They discussed the immortality of the soul.

In the midst of the most immediate problems, there are certain timeless questions which are always timely. Our attitude toward these eternal issues serves to steady or weaken our morale in facing current concerns. And for a proper relationship to contemporary affairs, perhaps nothing is more basic than a right adjustment to time itself.

The element of time is a very present one to most persons. Every modern contrivance seems conspiring to make us conscious of time. We live and move and have our being in the presence of clocks. The progressive shift of population from the soil to the city has transferred us from the timing of the seasons to the staccato of train schedules and ticker-tapes. And the spread of urban conditions to the country has brought the wages-

and-hours calculations to the farm. If we so enjoy our work that we never watch the clock, sooner or later we do look at the calendar. Even though buoyant health may make us smile at the passing years, competitive business all too soon reminds us that age does count. Children talk much about their birthdays, yet worry little about them. Their elders talk little about their age, yet worry much about it.

And having become time-conscious, most of us think of time as an enemy. We call him Father Time, but we picture him as a grim reaper with a scythe. This should not be so to those who have learned the mastery of life from the Great Teacher. The good life declares a truce with time, even transforming the enemy into an ally.

The first simple suggestion for this truce is to stop fighting time as if it were the foe of our usefulness. The desire to be of use is a major factor in making life worth living. The deepest need of our natures is to feel that we are needed. And to be sure, time does seem to put a terminus both to our marketable work and often to those personal responsibilities which make us feel that we are playing a vital part in the family or social group. In fact, our high-powered machine culture appears to make ever shorter the period of a man's productive years. Any person over forty knows the tragic realities of the dead-line set by age in the industrial world. One of the dilemmas of our day is that while our medical science is prolonging our years of possible activity, our economic science seems unable to find occupations for the years we are lengthening. Certainly the plainest of Christian duties is to do all in our power as a society to make old age secure.

But mere economic security is no satisfying answer to man's craving for life. It does not fulfill the wish to be of use. We are born with creative desires, and the strategy of living is to keep these functioning to the farthest reach of our years. These must therefore find scope in realms outside the office and factory, and then when age brings us to what is called retirement, we do not topple over like spinning tops which have run down. We can be kept going by finding a usefulness beyond the measure of the public marketplace.

When we leave the realm of commercial rewards and enter the sphere of values, there is no competition to crowd us out. There is no law of supply and demand to limit the production of beauty, truth, and goodness. One of the heartening phases of modern life is the new usefulness being discovered by middle-aged mothers after their child-rearing duties are done. Their activities are expanding into the realms of public service, adult education, the fine arts; and their earlier labors, which were assumed to leave our grandmothers exhausted and ready for the fireside nooks, are now being revealed as the means of enrichment for further service. Do not the experiences of motherhood sharpen the artistic insight and do not long years of human contact deepen the understanding essential to effective writing? Why should not tomorrow blossom with budding autumnal artists and writers to supplement the current vogue of youthfulness?

There is good precedent for predicting an extension of usefulness beyond the "dead-line" of age. Immanuel Kant was seventy-four when he wrote his "Metaphysics

of Ethics." Tintoretto was the same age when he painted
his vast canvas of "Paradiso." John Wesley, when past
eighty, was still preaching up and down England saying
with a smile, " 'Tis time to live if I grow old."

> Is it too late? Ah, nothing is too late
> Till the tired heart shall cease to palpitate.
> Cato learned Greek at eighty; Sophocles
> Wrote his grand "Oedipus" and Simonides
> Bore off the prize of verse from his compeers
> When each had numbered more than four score years.
>
> .    .    .
>
> Chaucer at Woodstock with the nightingales
> At sixty wrote the "Canterbury Tales."
> Goethe at Weimar, toiling to the last,
> Completed "Faust" when eighty years were past.
> These are indeed exceptions; but they show
> How far the Gulf Stream of our youth may flow
> Into the Arctic regions of our lives,
> Where little else than life itself survives.[1]

In answer to such a list it may be said that the citations
of genius do not help the situations of the commonplace.
Granted that not many of us can use our later years to
produce noteworthy creations of pen or canvas, usefulness is not confined to such spectacular contributions.
In mind at the moment is an unmarried aunt no longer
able to find commercial employment and not capable of
creating artistic things. Yet by her spirit of cheerful
fortitude and contagious coöperation, she is worth immeasurably much to both the younger and older members of the household. And do not most of us know some

[1] Longfellow, Henry W., "Morituri Salutamus."

elderly persons who stand serenely above the heat and tension of surface living, their white heads rendering to the circles around them a service comparable to the lift given by a snowclad peak to a traveler in the lowlands? They catch the first tints of the dawn and hold the lingering rays of the setting sun. These wise and godly elders anticipate the hopes of youth and lengthen the days of the adults. And from their summits of experience they catch the intimations of that larger life which "eye hath not seen, nor ear heard." [2] Yes, "They also serve who only stand and wait."

A second suggestion for a truce with time is to cease fighting age as if it were the foe of our pleasures. We take it for granted that we "must go it while we are young" and that, as Ecclesiastes put it, "the years draw nigh, when thou shalt say, I have no pleasure in them." [3] Admittedly youth has a tremendous capacity for pleasure. The young in their exuberance of energy rush from excitement to excitement. And in time such vitality does abate. But life has its seasonal compensations, and those who learn its rhythm find it no anticlimax to move from flaming youth to the thrifty, home-building thirties, the roaring forties, the full fifties and the serene sixties.

One of the compensations of time is that when it takes away youth it leaves memories which are even more pleasant than those early experiences were at the time. Thomas Carlyle once parried the question as to why the past looks so beautiful to us. In answer he suggested this reason: "It is because fear has been extracted from it, for

[2] I Corinthians 2: 9.
[3] Ecclesiastes 12: 1.

one thing." We see his point. When a pleasure is in prospect, we are disturbed by the fear that it may not be realized, but a pleasure in retrospect is secure. When we look back on the days of our youth, we tend to think of them as almost unalloyed delight. But they were not. They were filled with fears. Perhaps mine was a nature unduly disposed to worry, but I was wont to becloud the approach to a vacation or excursion by counting impatiently the days remaining until the big event. And then when I was on my vacation or excursion, I proceeded to count gloomily the dwindling number of days left to be enjoyed. Thus I tended to overshadow both the beginning and the end of many a good time. But now in my memory I dwell on those pleasant occasions without the accompanying shadows.

Yet the custodianship of memory is not an adequate preservative of pleasure. Too tame is it merely to contemplate our good times in retrospect. We must get a grip on our high moments which is not loosened by the passage of time. It would seem that our enthusiasms grow more short-lived as the tempo of living is speeded up. Whittier's barefoot boy seemed to get a longer enjoyment from his simple home-made playthings than does the modern lad from his elaborate amusement devices and ever-changing movies. And we adults are prone to neglect the lasting things in our search for the latest things. Sensations chase one another across the front pages of our papers, and no single event is spectacular enough to hold the public interest more than a few days. In trying to keep up to the minute, our interests tend to become momentary.

Vicki Baum in "Grand Hotel" graphically describes this elusiveness: "The real thing is always going on somewhere else. When you are young, you think it will come later. Later on, you think it was earlier. When you are here, you think it is there. But when you get there, you find that life has doubled back and is quietly waiting here, here in the very place you ran away from. It is the same with life as it is with the butterfly collector and the swallow tail. As you see it flying away it is wonderful. But as soon as it is caught, the colors are gone and the wings bashed."

The good life partakes of that spirit of sport which throws itself wholeheartedly into every game as if that were the sole object in life and yet is not undone by success or failure when the particular game is over. And how are we able to put ourselves wholly into the pleasures of the present and then to keep our hearts whole when those experiences are passed? By realizing that the sources of satisfaction are carried within our own spirits rather than in the things to be enjoyed. The relation of a joyous experience to a person is like that of the weight of a book to the earth. Where does the weight of the book reside? Well, we could change its weight without tearing a leaf from its pages if we could alter its relation to the earth. It is the force of the earth's gravity which helps to determine the weight of the book. It is the health of the eater which helps to make the food seem good. Obvious, even trite, as this truth is, most of us have not lived our way into it. We have not learned to transfer our treasures of pleasure from the external realm "where moth and rust doth corrupt and where thieves break through and steal." We have not appropriated the truth of the Kingdom of Heaven within us and thus beyond the reach of time's wear and tear.

When we have really learned this secret of the good life, we "have builded a house which is not for time's throwing." Time may have taken away the money which we had ten years ago; time removes from us the sports in which we were once able to indulge; age deprives us eventually of the travel we once relished. But when we take to heart the truth that "though the outer man perish, yet the inner man is renewed day by day," then time instead of impoverishing us enriches by capitalizing our past experiences. As our inner capital grows, our interest in the present increases. We are able to make more out of simple things. Well-ripened age gets far more joy out of a June day or an evening's conversation than does raw youth.

When I take a trip with my seventeen-year-old daughter, I enjoy the experience with more tenses than does she, for I have the present sensations provided by the sights we see, plus the memory of my own youthful trips with my father, plus the added insight which my wider travels have given me, plus the vicarious enjoyment which a parent gets from the pleasures of his child. Thus the added tenses of age more than match the intensity of youth.

Anatole France, in "The Garden of Epicurus," whimsically remarked that had he been given the privilege of creating man, he would have done so on the pattern not of the biped, but of the caterpillar, for the former starts life upright and then verges toward the earth, while the latter starts life horizontally but later wings its way upward. Physically, to be sure, we are bipeds, but spiritually we can live on an ascending scale.

And now a third suggestion for this truce with time. We should cease fighting time as the foe of our affections. So many of our books, motion pictures and common observations give the impression that love grows stodgy and tarnished with age.

The native passions do lose their ardor. The physical fuel which sustains "the flame of youth" is not inexhaustible. But the light which feeds from its own candle can with the passing years be changed into an incandescence whose radiance comes from a larger source. Yonder is an acquaintance now past eighty. Instead of the years causing a dimming of the lights, his is a case of lights coming on at eventide. He is alive at more points today than sixty years ago. The doctors have kept his body alive, but the Great Physician has kept his spirit alive—alive to the needs of others, alive to the bubbling joys of little children, alive to the appeal of art, alive to the call of world interests. The flame of youth has been transformed into the radiance of age.

Where is the most beautiful description of love we know? Speaking for myself, I find it in these well-known lines: "Love suffereth long and is kind; love envieth not; love vaunteth not itself, is not puffed up, doth not behave itself unseemly, seeketh not her own, is not easily provoked, thinketh no evil; rejoiceth not in iniquity, but rejoiceth in the truth; beareth all things, believeth all things, hopeth all things, endureth all things. Love never faileth." [4]

Now let us ask ourselves does this description fit young love or love that is matured? Is it true that young love "suffereth long and is kind"? I have seen some broken-hearted young lovers who did not suffer very long and some hot-headed youth who were cruel rather than kind in their zeal of love. Is it true that youthful love "envieth not"? I have seen some young suitors looking with green-eyed envy at their more successful rivals. Is it correct to say that young love "seeketh not its own"? What is more possessive than youthful love's passion for its object? Is it accurate to say of young love that it "is not easily provoked"? What could be more fiery and sensitive?

Perhaps we have looked far enough to see that the love Paul so beautifully describes is a mellowed, ripened affection, a passion made tolerant by the memory of past mistakes, made charitable by gratitude for past forgiveness? Love between man and woman is beautiful to behold at the marriage altar, but it has a richer sheen on a Golden Wedding anniversary. Love between friends has a rare fineness amid the enthusiasms of a college campus, but it has an added depth after long years of sharing common burdens and responsibilities. Social passion is splendid in the young idealist, but far more magnificent is it to keep the charitableness of brotherhood into a truly liberal old age. Love of God is a warming experience in the first flush of a youthful convert's zeal, but it is far more satisfying in the heart of a veteran, who after

[4] I Corinthians 13: 4–8.

long years in the service of his Lord can say: "I know whom I have believed, and am persuaded that he is able to keep that which I have committed unto him against that day." [5]

After a crushing political defeat, Gladstone on one occasion rose to speak with buoyant confidence, saying, "Time is on our side." We too may have time for an ally.

[5] II Timothy 1: 12.

# Chapter II

# TODAY IS OURS

TODAY is ours. But who says so? When we hear these words on the lips of a ne'er-do-well, we know that he is voicing the hand-to-mouth philosophy of short-sighted indolence which, like the tramp, begs the morsels of satisfaction at the backdoors of life. When an extravagant and indulgent monarch like Louis XV says, "Today is ours," he means that he will get while the getting is good and leave the payment to posterity, foreseeing as he said, "After us the deluge." When a bullying war lord has strained his nation's resources to the breaking point in order to bring his fighting forces to the peak of preparedness, he must rely on the quick thrust for he knows that time is against him. And Omar Khayyam is voicing the sensualist's feeling that only today is ours when he lifts his glass and sings:

> Some for the Glories of This World: and some
> Sigh for the Prophet's Paradise to come;
> Ah, take the Cash and let the Credit go,
> Nor heed the rumble of a distant Drum!

In all the above instances we see reflected the feeling that the present is the one secure possession between an unrecoverable past and an unpredictable future. Such is the mood which invades some minds in times of critical uncertainty. We saw it in Germany during 1922 when no one knew what the currency would be worth the next day. We see it in certain circles of American life today. During the past winter when the clouds of war rolled up over the horizon and the roads of business were in densest fog, New York had one of its gayest seasons. Not knowing what the day would bring forth, men made the most of their nights. When the past and future edges of the present are eaten away by uncertainty, indifference or any other time-unbinding attitude, the threads of purpose are loosened, morals become lax and the whole social fabric begins to unravel.

Yet on the other hand there is a sense in which we can say, "Today is ours," for the very reason that we do trust the tomorrows. The Master of Life demonstrated a way of living which did not sacrifice the present on the altar of the future. He did not rush through Palestine so bent on his mission that he could not enjoy the scenery along the way. He took time to stop and play with little children, to share the joys of festive occasions, to revel in the beauties of nature. He counseled against the practice of bankrupting our todays by paying interest on the regrets of yesterday and borrowing in advance the troubles of tomorrow.

How can we hold the present experience so that it does not run out on us, either backward in futile retrospect or forward in impotent longing? We do have moments in which we are wholeheartedly engrossed, in which we are "all there." Forgetful of time's passing we seek no future; we recall no past. "The present possesses us, though within this present our minds run back and forth as they do when we take in all at once the sounds, smells and colors of early morning at sea." [1] How to combine this absorption in the immediate with the continuity of growth—that is a task of the good life. Whereas he who lives for today seeks his thrills by cutting off thought of the future, he who lives for tomorrow tries to hold his high moments by tying the loose ends of the present into the texture of time. The commonest way of losing our todays is through their loose ends.

One set of loose ends through which our todays unravel is this: Questions opened and never closed. So apparent are the evils of the closed mind that we overlook the peril of the open mind. While we are surrounded by stubborn and prejudiced persons who close their minds and refuse to open them, we should also observe those who are better at opening their minds than at closing them. Yes, and we should note, too, that both tendencies may exist in the same person. An individual may be intolerant on some issues and liberal on others, his mind walled up on one side and a swinging door on the other.

Some keep their minds much too open on the rearward side. They continue to look back at yesterday's decisions, wondering whether they have reached the right conclusions and spending their energy in retrying cases. A popular essayist tells of a young minister who was so successful in his first parish that he received an invitation to another. But being firmly rooted in the affections of his people, he declined the call. Then his troubles began, for thereafter when anything went wrong he thought of the delightful church which he had refused.

[1] Cabot, Richard, "The Meaning of Right and Wrong." New York, Macmillan, p. 142.

Some years later he did take a new parish. Then after the excitement of moving was over, his troubles began again, for whenever any difficulty was encountered he thought of the "dear old place" he had left. Thus the poor fellow allowed the energy and enjoyment of the present to escape through the mental door left open in the rear. To-day's peace of mind is secured by closing the gate to keep out yesterday's yelping pack of hounding worries. To-day's executive efficiency depends on the ability to shut the door on yesterday's decisions. This is the truth which Jesus drove home by such remarks as, "No man, having put his hand to the plough, and looking back, is fit for the Kingdom of God," [2] or the sharper surgical one, "Let the dead bury their dead." [3]

Many husbands and wives have never really settled the question of their own marriage. They keep looking backwards, wondering if they might have done better, or they even continue to look around, wondering if they might still do better. A home never has a fair chance of succeeding unless those who take the vows of marriage regard them as final and try to make the most of the possibilities within those settled sidelines. Our minds are like cameras in that they must be closed in the rear and on the sides in order to take a picture of what is in front. And our spirits never bring their full reserves to the attack until they consciously and subconsciously burn their bridges behind them.

One of the aids to the efficient life is to reduce certain areas of activity to automatic action, so that our minds

[2] Luke 9: 62.
[3] Luke 9: 60.

are left free for the vital new decisions to be made. Did
the strong men who gave stability to the social, economic
and religious life of the nineteenth century have a larger
proportion of fixed habits and settled convictions than
we of the twentieth? In making a fetish of freedom we
have so striven to emancipate ourselves from our fathers'
fixed rules that about the only habit we cultivate is that
of not having any habits. When we hold a Hamlet's so-
liloquy over lines of behavior which should be taken for
granted, we waste the energy which should be given to
decisive objectives. Speaking as a religious liberal, I
would raise my voice for a revived study of the value of
vows and fixed rules. Some old questions must be closed
if the right new questions are to be raised.

A second set of loose ends through which we lose our
todays is this: Desires filled but not developed. There is
a proverb which reads thus: "The slothful man roasteth
not that which he took in hunting, but the substance of a
diligent man is precious." [4] Hunting is such a pleasurable
pursuit that even a slothful man will follow the chase.
But when the game has been caught, then the lazy
hunter leaves to the others the drudgery of dressing
and roasting it for food. And very often the camp of an
early huntsman was littered with the waste of that which
he had caught and not used.

Similarly in life, we join the chase for profits and possessions. We feel the zest of accumulation. And some of
us succeed in surrounding ourselves with rich collections.
But how often it happens that we lack the diligence to
extract from those possessions the true food of our minds

[4] Proverbs 12: 27.

and spirits. We avidly devour the current best sellers, but derive from them only a fraction of the stimulus which our fathers received from a few select volumes. Many of us read too much and think too little. The children of privilege frequently get less fun from their elaborate playground equipment than did the farm boy of former days from his few simple home-made playthings. Have we increased our resources and lessened our resourcefulness?

Lacking the diligence to make worthy use of what we have, we go on trying to accumulate more. George Tyrrell, the mystic, was wont to say that sensations can become the food of our souls, but to make them so, we need to lie down and ruminate on them, as do the cattle in the field. Yet this we do not do. We keep browsing over the green pastures of our rich modern world, ever restlessly gazing at greener fields beyond our reach. We seek quantity of sensation rather than quality of experience. During the booming 1920's one of our publicists thus described the stereotype of American ambition: Whatever is poor wants to be rich, whatever is slow wants to be fast, whatever is small wants to be large, whatever is wants to be more so.

Has the financial depression delivered us from this addition complex? Some signs are heartening. Many a parent who once was rich enough to do many things *for* his children is now learning to do more things *with* them. There is some evidence of a new appreciation of simple inexpensive pleasures. The momentary stringency is making us more sensitive to material waste. Our safety campaigns and our social legislation are arousing us to the prevention of human waste. It would certainly seem that all this should be paralleled by a new concern for the waste resulting from our tendency to collect without developing. There is a rising popular resentment against those who own without using. If this impatience be turned toward ourselves, we shall discover how our lives are littered like the camp of a lazy huntsman with heaps of half-used possessions. It may even cause us to ask whether we are sit-down strikers holding places in which others might be producing. Surrounded by unemployed who would like our jobs and by refugees who long for our citizenship, we should see that it is little short of criminal to waste the opportunities and privileges of the present.

Recently the press carried a picture of Helen Keller on a visit to the New York World's Fair. It was very startling: a woman without sight or hearing trying to appraise the vast presentation of tomorrow's mechanical wonders. And yet when I contrast the rich current of life which flows through her few physical senses with what I get through my five healthy ones, I feel like an amateurish village trap-drummer in the presence of a Paganini. With one or two strings she can make more melody than I can, surrounded by all my traps and devices. Perhaps Helen Keller's achievement of making so much out of so little, a feature neglected by the world of today, may be revived in the world of tomorrow.

A third set of loose ends through which our todays are running out on us is this: Impulses felt but not organized or controlled. Several factors have contributed to create the impulsive rather than the imperative mood.

For one thing our generation has been indoctrinated with the idea of self-expression as against self-repression. Rightfully reacting against old prohibitive rules, we have wrongly interpreted personal liberty. Following the slogan, "Obey that impulse," we have discovered that obedience to impulse is one of the worst forms of slavery. Many of us have allowed our momentary enthusiasms to carry us into a chaos of desired ends. Others of us live at inner cross purposes. The tensions of conflicting desires consume our energies and confuse our objectives. Still others of us become inconsistent in our self-control, being puritanically strict at some points and cavalierly lax at others. Much living is a series of clever by-plays with no main drive. A friend of mine, with a versatile mind and a varied education, well illustrates the waste due to inner disorganization. Lift any subject in his presence and his conversation flashes around it like heat lightning on a summer evening, but he has never struck anything. With all his brilliance, he has never set anything on fire. Or consider the large class of those whom Pearl Buck calls "gunpowder women," privileged, educated, potential, yet impotent because their energies are not fired toward any definite targets.

The task of personal integration grows ever more difficult. Our sympathies may well go out to the young as they face the task of finding a job and the still more difficult task of finding themselves in their jobs. With every line of work subdivided into intricate specialties and with every avenue crowded, the wonder is that more of our youth do not go to pieces. A wise and experienced counselor recently said that he would like to add to the college curriculum a chair to be known as "The Art of Facing Life," and the first course to be given in that department would be on "What to do when you have nothing to do." Training in such a course should precede technical skills. A youth does not need to wait to discover what kind of a job he wants or can get before he decides what kind of a person he wishes to be.

When Charles Kingsley visited Salisbury Cathedral, he wrote a letter to his wife describing the structure. He said that the lower part is broken up in the wildest confusion of towers until "its self-willed fancies exhaust themselves, and it makes one final struggle upward in a vast single pyramid, and when that has dwindled to a point, it ends in a cross." Kingsley's description of Salisbury Cathedral suggests a satisfying plan of life-building. Beautiful as is the lower structure, it is the central spire which gives distinction and lift to that shrine. So with our lives. When our self-willed fancies and our physical desires exhaust their impulsive energies, there is needed some central purpose, rising like a spire to give design and finish to our living.

Along with a unifying purpose should go a strengthening of ideals into standards, if we are to hold our todays. Since the World War we Americans have extended the range of our ideals as our farmers enlarged the area of arable land in the west. We think in large terms. We have wider aspirations for world peace, industrial justice, racial brotherhood, even on the eve of conflict. But the social result has been somewhat like the physical aftermath of the agricultural effort, namely, a dust bowl. Our ideals are characterized by a loose vagueness. They lack definite local applications. We leave so many issues half-decided. We do not clinch our convictions. Lives thus loosened easily drift in almost any direction. And the fertile soil from which enjoyment springs is soon gone with the wind. The qualities which make good starters are more prevalent today than those which make good finishers. Our quick impatient generation lacks the plodding perseverance and unflagging fortitude which sees life through. Some of us have many irons in the fire but we change them so often that only the handles get hot. We do not go after them "hammer and tongs" to weld them into something useful. The cult of comfort predisposes us to postpone the difficult tasks while we dally with the more pleasant. The late Doctor Richard Cabot of Harvard laid down a personal formula worth considering as a corrective for this tendency to leave hard jobs unfinished. He writes: "I think the element of self-deception is almost always there when one procrastinates. For one does not refuse the disagreeable job once for all. It is not definitely repudiated; it is accepted as a proper claim, some time,—only not just now. When I am in any doubt about whether such a plea is true I ask myself, 'Can you name another time that will really be any better than this? If so mark it down in black and white. Let someone else know about it, and if possible, remind you of it when the time comes.' If I cannot name such a right time I diagnose the case as self-deception and stand self-condemned to immediate performance." [5]

Yes, today is ours to be possessed to the full. But since

[5] Cabot, Richard, "The Meaning of Right and Wrong." New York, Macmillan, p. 294.

we are "such stuff as dreams are made of," we cannot treat the present as an island of sense experience surrounded by an ocean of forgetfulness. Today is an isthmus connecting the continents of memory and hope.

*Chapter III*

# LIVE FOR TOMORROW

A SOCIAL worker recently reported a survey made of American youth. As a result of his contact with twenty thousand young people, the speaker gave the following findings: Of the youth out of school and in the labor market, three out of ten are unemployed; forty-three per cent of those who have work feel themselves to be in dead-end jobs; the younger generation today is more concerned with security than adventure, and is "preoccupied with the unromantic business of tomorrow's board and room." [1]

However loose such a generalisation may be, it indicates that youth is now in a condition wherein it will not long remain. The mind of youth is made to be the home of ideals and hopes, and cannot be healthily transformed into a rooming house outside of which is hung the sign, "Board by the day or week." It was youth in such a disillusioned state that Lenin caught in Russia, Mussolini caught in Italy, and Hitler in Germany. Who or what will catch our younger generation?

We are designed to live for tomorrow. We cannot hold the present and the present cannot hold us. It is true, today is ours and we should live it to the full. We were not intended to dash through the present like the Twentieth Century Limited, ignoring the way stations in our haste to reach the terminal of some Utopia. But there is

[1] *New York Times*, May 17, 1939.

23

a difference between living today and living for today. The strategy of the good life is in capitalizing today's wealth of experience for tomorrow's interest.

It is hardly necessary to stimulate interest in the future. Skeptical of tomorrow we may be, but not indifferent. It is doubtful if any previous generation strained so hard to get a preview of what is ahead. These words are being written in a city where one hundred and fifty-five millions of dollars have been expended to devise an Exposition which depicts the "World of Tomorrow." We have flocked to view its futuramas with their portrayal of tomorrow's traffic, tomorrow's houses of mechanical magic, tomorrow's wizardry of light. We are more eager than were the ancients to peer over the threshold of the yet-to-be. Whereas Saul consulted the witch of Endor and the Greeks journeyed to the oracles at Delphi and elsewhere, we turn to the physical scientists for tomorrow's weather, to the economists for tomorrow's business, and to the press columnists for the prediction of tomorrow's trends. The faster we live, the more impatient we are to see what is ahead.

Yet with all our eagerness to foresee the future, we fail sadly in our design for living toward it. Youth, impatient to overtake tomorrow, so often tries to capture in the teens the thrills that normally come in the twenties. And middle age, the most dangerous period of life, becomes engrossed in the immediate and mundane to the neglect of the invisible and eternal. The middle years seem least responsive to religious appeal. At this period there is less service given to social enterprises. From thirty to fifty men are so busy trying to get ahead personally that they give little aid to helping public enterprises. The dominance of the "Old Guard" in church circles and political parties is usually due to the indifference of the middle-aged more than to the tenacity of the aged. It would seem that the prophet Joel had significance in his omission when he wrote, "Your old men shall dream dreams, your young men shall see visions." [2] The spiritual illumination seems to miss the middle-aged.

As life advances toward the sunset it tends to catch the glow of the light beyond the horizon, but all too often the interest of old age in the future is compensatory rather than constructive. And sometimes our elders try to recapture the thrills they think they have missed by a a kind of silly second childhood of artificial youthfulness.

If we would live for tomorrow, we must learn the truly provident life. For this we recall no better formula than that given by the veteran Paul to young Timothy in his counsel of "laying up in store for themselves a good foundation against the time to come." [3] The first impact of those words may be to turn the reader's thought to life after death. But the Master whom Paul served did not divide life by the boundary of the grave. Eternal life, as taught by Jesus, is a quality of living which continues through the incident of death. In preparing for the future we may adopt in all seriousness the sign read by a certain tourist of which President Conant of Harvard tells. This motorist, having been forced to detour, came to an uninviting stretch of unimproved road, at the entrance to which had been placed this no-

[2] Joel 2: 28.
[3] I Timothy 6: 19.

tice: "Choose well your rut, for you will be in it a long time." Similarly, we fashion here the quality of life which carries through into the long tomorrow.

We are to live a cumulative life. As the bee stores honey for the days when the flowers are gone, so with man the present should produce a surplus. The virtue of thrift is basic to the good life and needs emphasis in our day. This of course can lead to a niggardly, miserly, materialistic spirit of hoarding. But real life cannot be hoarded. The Silas Marners counting their golden piles and the chronic invalids coddling their strength lose out as did the rich shortsighted farmer in the gospel parable. The cautious calculators with their bird-in-the-hand maxims miss the melody of the birds in the bushes. The truly provident life, as advocated by Paul, is laid on a principle of generous spending, "rich in good works, ready to distribute, willing to communicate." [4] Nor is such generosity motivated by a self-centered desire to store up merit in heaven.

There is a provident way of living which is not niggardly, prudent nor selfishly otherworldly, but is practical, present and eternal. When, for instance, we spend our strength properly, we store up strength. When we expend our mental energy in healthful study, even in straining effort, we increase the potency of our intellectual processes, although some college students, we confess, seem to proceed on the principle of saving their intellectual strength until they leave the campus. When we pour out love toward wholesome objects, we find our capacity for love expanding. "Love suffereth long and

[4] I Timothy 6: 18.

is kind . . . beareth all things, believeth all things, hopeth all things, endureth all things." [5] And having done all this, love is then exhausted? Ah, no. "Now abideth faith, hope, love." [6] These abide only with those who spend them.

Our spirits seem adjusted to our bodies somewhat as the batteries are attached to our motor cars. If properly regulated they are stored by running. Observe the spiritually exhausted persons around us—and they are legion —tired liberals, pent-house socialists, youthful cynics. Many there are who bemoan that men are morons, that people have lost the willingness to work, that the young are worse than their fathers, but do we find the veteran social workers and teachers in this chorus of complaint? Those who have spent most in the service of men, still retain most faith in human nature. Those who, through long suffering or severe hardships, would seem to have most reason to lose faith in God's providence are the firmest believers.

There is a way of living by a law of increasing dividends; there is another way of living by a law of diminishing returns. When we depend on artificial stimulants, we must keep stepping up the dose to get the same "kick"; when we live by natural satisfactions, drawing on our own resources, we get growing enjoyments from the same stimuli. Sunsets do not have to be stepped up to hold the interest of one who loves nature. The good life draws increasing returns from simple things. Tastes find more and more subtle satisfactions. After a night of sensual

[5] I Corinthians 13: 7.
[6] I Corinthians 13: 13.

indulgence there is the "morning-after" feeling of exhausted thrills, but he who has learned the deeper joys sings "New every morning is thy love."

If we are to live for tomorrow, we must learn the difference between spendthrift living which impoverishes, and the thrifty spending of life which results in "laying up in store for themselves a good foundation against the time to come."

And note secondly what is to be laid up—a *good foundation*. It is not courageous to ask for a guaranteed future. Foolish would be the father who said to his son, "I have made your financial future secure so that you will always be cared for." Such a guarantee would likely remove the backbone from the lad as neatly as one removes it from a fish. But the wise father does endeavor to give his child the security of a good foundation. He undergirds the infant feet with trustworthy parental love. He trains the tender vine of childhood traits upward on the framework of a solid home with the strong ties of family loyalty, thereby imparting to the growing spirit a sense of security so sadly lacking in the children of homes broken by divorce or death. How often we hear parents in modest circumstances say: "We have no fortune to leave our children, but we are going to give them a good home and a good education, and then they will be able to fend for themselves." And thus they give them the best of all fortunes—"a foundation." And children have no right to ask for more.

By the same logic governments should seek to emphasize for their citizens the economic security of foundations rather than of fortunes. My country does not owe me a living, but it does owe me a society in which I can make a living. As a citizen I have no right to ask my government to bear my personal burdens for me, but I have a right to look to my government for the law and order which enable me to bear my own burdens in those things which a person can do for himself, and for leadership and foresight in planning those larger services which we can only do together. The function of good government is not to soften its citizens with guaranteed futures, but to strengthen them with secure foundations on which they can build their own tomorrows.

One of our troublous tendencies in facing the future is to look for shelter rather than for foundation. This is partly due to our shortsighted self-protectiveness and partly to our impatience to see the finished structure, before we lay the foundation. We have a curiosity to peek at the last page to see how things are coming out before we learn the first lessons. When I began the study of plane and solid geometry, I thumbed idly through the back pages until my eye caught the drawing of a parallelopipedon with its elaborate and confusing lines of explanation. The sight of that perplexing figure was nearly fatal to my interest in geometry. I said, "This is too much for me." But when, under the teacher's guidance, I turned the first pages and learned the simple axioms, I gradually worked my way up to a comprehension of those complex propositions at the end of the book.

This principle of approach is one to be applied in all our problems. The Master used it in dealing with his disciples' previews of the future. When the mother of Zebedee's children came with her two sons asking that they be given prime places in the kingdom which Christ was to set up, Jesus answered, "Ye know not what ye ask. Are ye able to drink of the cup that I shall drink of and to be baptized with the baptism that I am baptized with?" [7] He took their eyes off the final rewards and focused them on the first requirements.

Again, when the Fourth Gospel in the matchless fourteenth chapter reports the Master's promise of a place which he was to prepare for his followers, it interprets Jesus as saying, "Whither I go ye know, and the way ye know." Whereupon Thomas countered, "Lord, we know not whither Thou goest, and how can we know the way?" To this Jesus replied, "I am the way, the truth, and the life." The doubting disciples were to cease puzzling themselves as to how the future life was coming out and fasten their thought on how it was going in.

Living today seems as complicated as the movements of a centipede. But, after all, we are only bipeds and not centipedes, and most of us are intelligent enough to know which foot to start on. If we put our better foot forward on the immediate duty which we can see, we shall be surprised to discover how our vision clears. In our social situations today we are like the American soldiers in the army camps during the World War who were impatient to move up to the front line trenches but were loath to do the squad drills. We are eager to attack the front line problems of war, industrial inequity and racial injustice. Youth cheers these ideals at high school commencements and in college chapels. But we are short on the local drill grounds. The defeats and casualties in

[7] Matthew 20: 22.

our large social programs may be traced in major part to lack of training in personal discipline and in local community enterprises. In fact society's present chaos is partly a form of moral and social awkwardness.

And now a third suggestion. If we are to lay up a good foundation on which the future can build, we must be prepared for the best as well as for the worst.

It is small wonder that the present world situation should create a crisis-psychology and a crisis-theology. It is not surprising that believers in Christ's second coming should find multiplied evidences that we are now in "the last days," that the Lord has exhausted his patience with perverse men and is about to come in cataclysmic fashion to wind up the present age. Those of us who do not hold these apocalyptic expectations, but who believe that Christ's way, as given on Calvary, cannot be improved upon as a means of saving our world—even we must admit that the future is pregnant with crisis. Great forces are clashing with convulsive results. Certain present trends cannot continue even another decade without some decisive change.

It is safe to predict that we Americans will be involved either in a war or in a peace movement far surpassing in intensity anything yet attempted. Suppose that war does come and finds us of those who believe it justifiable to fight for endangered ideals. Are we prepared to go through such a war, thrusting bayonets into the bodies of men and bombing babies in their beds, without losing more ideals than we save? Or if we are of those who refuse to kill even under the guise of war, are we prepared to be called "yellowbacks," to be ostracised by friends and clubs, perhaps to be interned in concentration camps and subjected to the indignities heaped upon conscientious objectors during the last war?

And war is only one form of crisis which the future may hold in store. When Mr. H. G. Wells portrayed "The Shape of Things to Come," he pictured the ideal society which is to be set up in the year 2059 A. D. It is to be a world of wonders with education so perfected that government will be unnecessary; with engineering so developed that instead of having to go to the mountains for summer coolness, climate can be improved by elevating mountain ranges in our midst; with collective ownership so organized that men can travel without luggage, claiming supplies and lodging wherever they go.

In all this Mr. Wells is spinning the web of imagination but he is doing so from strands of tendency already apparent. Education must be widened to relieve the mounting burden of governmental overhead. Unless men can be trained in socialized self-control, our increasing social controls will bankrupt us financially and destroy our liberties. Are we laying foundations for tomorrow in line with such a trend?

Engineering will be so improved that life will be easier physically. The preview of comforts promised by science for the World of Tomorrow makes the imagination dizzy. But as life grows easier physically, it becomes harder morally, with its lengthening leisure to be filled and its unspent physical energy to be channeled. What did the farmer or blacksmith of seventy-five years ago want when he finished his twelve or fourteen hours of toil in the shop or field? He desired rest and solitude and sleep. What does the office-worker or factory-worker of today wish when he or she gets through at four or five o'clock in the afternoon? Rest and solitude? Not at all. He wants excitement, entertainment, thrill. This surplus emotional and physical steam cannot be throttled down by social restraints and moral prohibitions. We must provide some wholesome outlets for this excess of energy which the ease of living is releasing, for our society may be undone by the misuse of its leisure as surely as by the mismanagement of its labor.

Although Mr. Wells' picture of the extent to which collective ownership will be carried seems fantastic, the limits of it are beyond prediction. At present we turn to government for the control of our misfortunes, such as floods, diseases, poverty, and their like, while we try to retain control of our good fortunes. As one interpreter has said, the American state is a "commonillth" rather than a "commonwealth." But when governmental agencies are called in to handle our ills, the way is being widened for their coming in to handle our weal.

Such trends as these are discernible in "the shape of things to come." Living for tomorrow involves laying foundations in line with these. But before these are consummated in a Utopia, Mr. Wells reminds us that society must undergo a holocaust of suffering involving a breakdown of finance and morale, a great wave of crime, destructive wars in the Far East and in Europe, and a depopulation of the world to one-half its members through pestilence. Fanciful? Again, a spinning of discernible strands.

In a time so electric as ours, crises can come "as the

lightning cometh out of the east, and shineth even unto the west." [8] In a world as interrelated as ours, crises may come as a flood, to use another of the Master's symbols, for floods are caused not merely by the storms which drench our district, but also by those which strike regions draining into ours. In "Vein of Iron" Ellen Glasgow makes her central figure say, as she beholds the entire family affected by her tragedy, "That is the greatest injustice in life—we cannot suffer anything alone, not even disgrace."

We must be prepared for both the lightning changes and the swelling floods. Against such contingencies little petty prudences are of small avail. When floods come we cry with the Psalmist, "Lead me to the rock that is higher than I." [9] No man has more religion than he can command in an emergency. Professor Peabody of Harvard was wont to say that the heroism of the moment, the doing of the noble and brave thing in the hour of crisis, is the result of long discipline. One of the basic differences between a truly religious man and a non-religious one is that the former faces his crises easily because he has prepared himself in advance, while the latter takes crises hard because he has been living easily and thoughtlessly beforehand.

Yet while we should be ready for emergencies "if worst comes to worst," we should not allow the gloomy expectation to cast its shadows over today. The good sailor does not permit the thought of tomorrow's storm

[8] Matthew 24: 27.
[9] Psalms 61: 2.

at sea to spoil the pleasure of today's shore leave. The Master of Life set his face steadfastly toward Jerusalem with its foreseen perils, but he did not let the shadow of the cross mar the radiance of his fellowship. The predominant note in Jesus' forecast of life was joy not sorrow "who for the joy that was set before him endured the cross." [10] He prepared for the best.

There is a very real sense in which preparation for the best proves the best preparation for the worst. When a person is constantly picturing to himself the worst possibilities, he weakens his power of meeting them. He lowers his resistance in advance. Tougher souls may steel themselves saying, "If worst comes to worst, I can stand it." But merely being able to "stand it" is not very victorious living. The really testing question is, "Can you make it?" Great characters do more than stand and take it; they take and make it—make their vicissitudes into victories, coming out of their trials "more than conquerors."

This triumphant living is partly the result of preparing for the best rather than for the worst. Such an attitude creates a victory complex whose potency is immeasurable, "able to do exceeding abundantly above all that we ask or think according to the power that worketh in us." [11] What we hold in the forefront of our thought has an uncanny way of driving us toward it.

Moreover, by preparing for the best we bring out the best in others. At present we are living on the defensive,

[10] Hebrews 12: 2.
[11] Ephesians 3: 20.

both as nations and as individuals. We suspect sinister motives even under every show of kindness. The propertied classes see a red menace around every corner, and the cry of fascism is heard on every side. We are like motorists who approach every corner with the foot on the brakes because we distrust the signal lights.

The evils of this defensive living are cumulative. Distrust begets distrust and then poisons both possessors. The person who knows he is under suspicion is never quite himself. He acts a bit queerly and thus tends to confirm the dark doubts about himself. In this way the shadows of suspicion thicken into the clouds of open strife.

In such a prevailing mood to prepare for the best rather than the worst would bring the impact of the unexpected. With our nerves on edge and our fists clenched, we are prepared to strike back—but if someone turned the other cheek, we should be taken off our guard as was Jean Valjean's sullen spirit when the good old bishop brought the other candlestick to match the one stolen.

In August, 1914, when the British Foreign Minister announced to the House of Commons his fateful declaration, he said that the nations had plenty of machinery for war but none for peace. Four years later at Versailles, the victorious nations revealed that they were still preparing for the worst rather than for the best. In revenge and greed was laid a foundation for the time to come. The time came. And the results may be read in the ruins. Will the rape of Poland, like that of Belgium, beget another child of the devil to repeat the vicious circle of destruction twenty years hence? We must either learn the true way of living for tomorrow or western civilization before the end of the century will be living on its yesterdays.

# Chapter IV

# LIFE'S GROWING EDGE

In his "Conquest of Happiness" Bertrand Russell suggests that we observe the eyes of the apes when we next take our children to the zoo. When these animals are not engaged in cracking nuts or performing gymnastic tricks, their eyes reflect a strange sadness. One can almost imagine that they feel they ought to become men but cannot discover the secret of how to do it. On the road of evolution they have lost their way. Their cousins marched on and they were left behind. Something of the same strain and anguish, says Russell, seems to have entered the soul of civilized man. He knows there is something better than himself almost within his grasp, yet he does not know where to seek it or how to find it.

Yes, there is a widespread awareness that the human race has missed its way. We have lost the trails to democracy and peace on which we thought ourselves twenty years ago. The business depression has made us vociferously conscious of our material losses. And those who do not think of themselves as lost souls headed for hell readily admit they have lost the clues to life's larger meanings.

Yet the most dangerous losses are those which we suffer without knowing it at the time. A person knows when he has lost his wealth; he does not always know when he has lost an opportunity. He knows when he has lost a loved one; he is not always aware when he has lost his own lovableness. He knows when he has lost his physical appetite; he may not be alert to the loss of his spiritual taste. The scales tell us when our bodies have stopped growing; but what informs us when our minds have ceased to grow?

We are born by degrees and we die by degrees. Growing life is a succession of new births—from the illiteracy of childhood into the world of letters, from the jungle of jazz and vagrant tunes into the realms of symphonies and concertos, from the isolations of single life into the shared joys of marital union, from the mundane interests of material living into the widened sympathies and heavenly hopes of the spiritual life. Occasionally these new births come with almost earthquake suddenness, but more often entrance into a new stage of life is gradual, like the dawning of a new day; and, as Edmund Burke said, we cannot draw a definite line between day and night although light and darkness are the exact opposites.

And life may depart by the imperceptible degrees of setting dusk. We say of a person in the grip of some progressive disease that he is "dying by inches"; yet there are other forms of slow death besides that of gradual physical decay. Walt Whitman once looked down with his compassionate heart at the body of a soiled woman of the city streets and exclaimed:

Dead house of love—house of madness and sin, crumbled, crushed.
House of life, erstwhile talking and laughing—but ah, poor house, dead even then.

In the life of the human spirit the slow changes need more to be watched than the sudden shocks. To be sure, we do have some sins which break out like measles in a single night. But the seven deadly sins, according to Roman Catholic tradition, suggest slow decay rather than sudden outbreak. Note the list: pride, covetousness, lust, envy, anger, gluttony, and sloth. These are evil tendencies which gradually harden the arteries of the spirit and sap the energies of the will. And note, too, that the most subtly dangerous of these are the sins which beset the mind rather than the body. Our bodily vices have a way of begetting their own punishment by eventually advertising themselves openly. Lust brings the disordered life and the disreputable career. Drunkenness leaves the bleary eye and the weakened frame. But the sins of the mind, like envy, prejudice, intolerance, may be carried around by the eminently respectable, concealed from the public, even from the possessor.

Look at the edges of your own life. Are they growing or dying? Behold the juncture of the generations. When we confront any entrenched social evil, we say cynically, "You can't teach an old dog new tricks. Our only hope is in the education of the young." But, alas, before our secular and religious schools can teach the young dogs new tricks, they have copied the ways of their elders. When adults create an atmosphere of vulgarity or vice or militarism or race hatred, the children absorb it despite the pious or pretty teaching of the schools. Our indirect education is so much more continuous and pervasive than our formal schooling and has been immeasurably enlarged by the motion picture and the radio.

Since we cannot break the vicious circles of social habit between generations, the hope of reform lies in teaching the old dogs some new tricks. Can this be done? A few years ago Professor Thorndike of Columbia made some tests to measure the ability of adults to learn new facts and new skills. His conclusion was that their "ability to learn is very nearly the same as the ability of youngsters between seventeen and nineteen years of age." Yet while adults can keep a growing edge, what is being done to keep it? Religious education scarcely reaches beyond the teen age, except such as may be derived from Sunday preaching, and since the Protestant average of church attendance is one Sunday in three and since the teaching content of the typical sermon is none too high, it is clear that the church is only playing with the problem of adult training.

As for secular adult education, much is being said on the subject today, but only a few communities are taking it seriously. So many of us take our college courses by a kind of cistern method, that is, we keep our minds more or less open during the semester to catch the ideas which drip off the eaves of the teachers' minds, and then at examination time we drop down an examination paper to measure the amount of factual information in our mental containers. But with it all, we tap no artesian springs of intellectual or cultural interest to keep us studying after the college years are over. The test of an educated person is in the mental alertness which he maintains through middle age and beyond. And if parents were strictly honest they would have to admit that one reason—though of course not the only reason—why youngsters do not stay more in the home is that the elders have not kept abreast of the growing mental interests of their children.

To maintain life's growing edge demands more than taking adult courses in art or literature or public affairs; more than women's clubs and town halls. It means, for one thing, keeping the mind free from fixed aversions and narrowing prejudices. Prejudice is a sin which all of us denounce and few of us seriously confess. It is hard to dislodge because the possessor does not admit, or often even know, that he has it. It is this self-deception and self-satisfaction which make prejudice so subtly sinister.

Whence come these prejudices which plague us and so seriously threaten the peace of society? It would seem at times that they are formed out of thin air. As was said by one of its victims, "Prejudice like the spider, makes everywhere its home, and lives where there seems nothing to live on." Yet when we look more closely, we discover some materials out of which these unreasoned dislikes are woven. One source is our inheritance. True is the old saying that we are tattooed in our cradles with the beliefs of our tribe. Infants absorb impressions before they are old enough to reason them out and subsequent education often only serves to rationalize their childish dislikes. To eradicate prejudice, therefore, we must reach back into the home. In the bosom of the family we bring out both our best and our worst. I recall a home where the attitude toward a colored employee delivered the children from any tendency to race prejudice and where a mother's intelligent interest in foreign missions freed the family from any anti-foreigner complex. In a public forum recently a thoughtful mother raised the question, "How can we guard children from race prejudice?" About the best answer is, "Start with the grandfathers." But grandfathers are so grievously hard to start.

In addition to inheritance a second source of fixed aversions is inertia. We dislike to change our minds. Although we are pathetically eager for new things and a fad is quickly popular, prophets are still stoned and pioneers are still ridiculed. We hate to be disturbed in our settled grooves of thought, and especially so if we are of those who have attained our place in the sun. When in the minority, men plead for tolerance and change, but when they become the majority they settle into rigid intolerance. Thus the established Puritans of Massachusetts Bay pushed out Roger Williams, and the Daughters of the American Revolution became the arch conservatives of the country their fathers fought to free.

How are set minds to be stirred from their inertia? Sometimes it is a case of the climate changing until the die-hards, like the dinosaurs, do not survive. Sometimes it happens that parents are liberalized by their children. The modern mother and father wish to keep young, and the cultivation of youthfulness may spread from the body to the mind. I have known more than one case of prejudice-reducing through mental massage by a progressive daughter, and more than one son who has helped to "bring up father" to a new viewpoint.

The hope of opening closed minds lies through personal influence rather than through direct propaganda. Men are steeled against efforts to put something over on them, but they are increasingly susceptible to style and fashion. The mental attitudes of a whole community can be broadened by the presence of a few liberal style-setters. One of the dangers at this point lies in the fact that the educated have been made so aware of propaganda that they are skeptical of everything they hear or read, while the less literate can be swayed by every demagogue and charlatan. Thus the inertia of the intelligent gives freer scope to the passions of the ignorant.

And it is amazing what areas of ignorance lie within the minds of seemingly cultivated folk. Good-will forums of Roman Catholics, Protestants and Jews have now become popular. And yet in these groups which pride themselves on their culture and tolerance, it is frequently confessed that what each knows about other faiths is derived from writers of his own sect, and all too often from anonymous documents at that. Until we are willing to seek information from the other side of our social fences, we cannot lay claim to open-mindedness.

If we are to keep life's growing edge, our imaginations must be quickened as well as our minds opened. In Bernard Shaw's "Joan of Arc" one of those who sent Joan to the stake confesses afterward that he had done a very cruel thing because he had not realized what cruelty was until he saw a young girl burning to death. Whereupon the Bishop of Beauvais exclaims, "Must then a Christ perish in torment in every age to save those that have no imaginations?" So it seems. It takes imagination to see the implications beyond the horizons of the immediate and also to get under the skin of the beholder. So many easy-going good persons say glibly that all our complex social problems could be solved if we would only practice the Golden Rule of doing unto another as we would that he should do unto us; but the trouble is that most people have not sufficient imagination to know what they would wish done to them if they were in the other fellow's place. The result is that well-intentioned people do unto others what they think is good for them, and that usually irritates them. Even the Golden Rule, practiced without imagination, is often sheer irritation.

In this matter of quickening the imagination, religion can and does play a potent part. When worshipers look up in prayer to God the Father of all mankind, it is like looking up into a mirror in the ceiling of a room. The reflection from the ceiling enables us the better to see down into the other person's place. One of the most intelligent and understanding world-citizens of my acquaintance is a woman who has never traveled five hundred miles from New York. Yet through her missionary interests, her personal contacts with foreign students in this country, her deep religious insight which beholds every person as of God-given worth, this little lady knows realistically how life looks to the person whose skin is black or whose residence is in Peiping, Prague or Tokyo. With her imagination she enters into the situations of others as did the Master who so identified himself with the poor, the sick, the outcast that he could say, "Inasmuch as ye have done it unto one of the least of these my brethren, ye have done it unto me." [1] Such sensitivity of imagination is not developed by occasional shocks any more than a compass is kept accurate by shaking. Of course our eyes are opened by an outrage

[1] Matthew 25: 40.

against the Jews in Berlin or a bombing of innocents in Warsaw. But if our insights are to be sharpened and lengthened into effectiveness, they require regular systematic cultivation, such as is given by repeatedly playing the moral searchlight of the prophets and the Christ on the problems of our human relationships. This is a function of true religion.

Nerves as well as imagination need quickening if life is to keep its growing edge. When we lose our nerve we are on the road to decay. Loss of nerve may be occasioned by various causes. It may come in a crisis as it came to Joseph Conrad's "Lord Jim," and the memory of a white feather shown in the dark night of danger may haunt our minds and weaken our morale through the long tomorrows. It may come through compromise with one's crowd as it overtook a certain young lawyer of this city. He came from a godly home in the middle west, and from a college campus where idealism ran high. He came with a conscience as sensitive as a kodak which could take a snapshot of a moral wrong. But now his conscience has grown so dull that he can take a time exposure of the most flagrant evil and register only a dull impression. He merely shrugs his shoulders and says "everybody does it."

Or loss of nerve may show itself in an unwillingness to dare the difficult. Lord Melbourne's cynical advice, "Do not try to do good and then you will not get into scrapes," was a revelation that he had lost his nerve. He might not have recognized his ailment as that, for we have such clever ways of rationalizing. We often call it being practical or tactful or diplomatic. Thus we shrink into our protective shell of prudence when we should be stepping forth boldly to dare the right and resist the wrong. Harold Begbie gave a devastating characterization of a former British premier by bidding his readers to compare the early portraits of the lean ascetic, fearless face of the young public man with the photographs of his later years, and then to ask whether they could expect the spirit behind those flaccid elderly features to lead in any crusade to make the kingdom of God prevail.

Still worse it is when we lose our sensitivity in feeling as well as our courage in daring. When we no longer feel a twinge of conscience at evils that once would stir us, when we no longer are disturbed by the joy of elevated thoughts at sights which once would have thrilled us—then we should know that we are losing our nerve. And the end of that process is the "unpardonable sin" against the Holy Spirit, unpardonable because we become so callous that we no longer feel the prick of conscience and hence do not turn to repentance.

"To be aware of one's virtue is to be a prig. To be aware of one's learning is to be a pedant. To wallow in one's pleasures is to be a hog. Prig, hog, and pedant are mired in their own attainments, trapped in the cave where they meant only to camp over night." [2] Who or what can dig us out of these stopping places and start us toward life's growing edge? Friends, of course, quicken our incentives, arouse jaded appetites, and stir up drowsy ambitions. In Cronin's "The Citadel," the faithful young

[2] Cabot, Richard, "The Meaning of Right and Wrong." New York, Macmillan, p. 144.

wife says to the slipping husband: "Don't you remember how you used to speak of life, that it was an attack on the unknown, an assault uphill—as though you had to take some castle that you knew was there but couldn't see, on the top?" The husband replied, "I was young then —foolish. That was just romantic talk." Nevertheless the wife's faith eventually helped to call the doctor back to his youthful ideals.

Also the examples of the heroic dead affect us as they did the young Greek when he cried, "The trophies of Miltiades will not let me sleep." It is heartening therefore to note a revival of hero-worship in the presentation of our current publications and motion pictures, especially in the field of Americana. These heroic lives make us realize that social progress has been due to those who pushed the growing edge of life beyond the bounds of conventional decency—to a Francis of Assisi who leavened the soddened mind of the Middle Ages by a love for lepers and outcasts, to a John Howard who aroused complacent England to the evils of the prison hells, to a Lord Shaftesbury who went beyond his own social group to lift the underprivileged, to a Florence Nightingale who defied convention to start a movement which healed men and freed women. When we are inclined to settle back content just "to be decent and let the devil take the hindmost," we are reminded by the testimony of history that if all our ancestors had lived on that level there would be no place today where the decent could be content. Progress demands something more dynamic than mere decency, something more redemptive than mere respectability.

And that something more has been supplied in immeasurable degree by the Carpenter of Nazareth. He lures minds out of their mediocrity by the perfection of his own personality. He saves the weak from settling back into despair and he safeguards the strong against the deceit of their own strength. He makes rich young men feel that they are missing something and he makes tarnished Magdalenes feel that they have not lost everything. By the winsomeness of his tolerance he sends the light of his spirit through the crevices of narrow minds and by the warmth of his passion he keeps broad minds from losing their convictions. He transforms the restlessness of worldliness into a divine discontent. He takes the tramp who is a wanderer because he is too lazy to dig himself in and makes him into the pioneer who moves to a new situation because he is energetic enough to dig himself out. The Christ channels change into progress. More than any other force in history he maintains life's growing edge.

# Chapter V

# HIGHWAYS OF HOPE

A ZIONIST Congress in Geneva has just been hearing the same call with which Zechariah stirred his disheartened and scattered countrymen: "Turn you to the stronghold, ye prisoners of hope." [1] Through the intervening centuries the Jewish people have been held in the grip of their great dream of a homeland.

Yet are we not all "prisoners of hope"? Who has not been caught by some dream which refuses to let him go? Hope can lure us forth like a Pied Piper and then turn to kidnap us. Hope can come in the guise of a liberator and then become our jailer.

When we lift our eyes from the personal to the world scene, we see the great expectations which have gripped us during the last two decades. Twenty years ago we reveled in the hope of a warless world, and now millions of men are marching in Europe—far more than were under arms in that fatal August of 1914. Twenty years ago we were dreaming of a world safe for democracy, and now dictators are trying to frighten free nations into a corner. Fifteen years ago we were entering the "golden glow" of Coolidge prosperity, and now ten or twelve million American citizens and billions of American dollars are keeping company in idleness unable to help one another. And yet we are still imprisoned by those hopes of peace and freedom and prosperity. Hav-

[1] Zechariah 9: 12.

ing been held under their spell, we cannot cut loose from them without feeling the heart go out of life.

But to what stronghold can we prisoners of hope turn to fortify our faith? Where are the roads to confidence for the realist? In the wilderness of world conditions there are no broad highways of hope visible to my eye. But there are trails which give promise. And the task of our generation, as of every other, is to take the pilgrim paths and broaden them into public highways, so that tomorrow's crowd may move up to the position of yesterday's pioneers and prophets. Although Hitler has set the spark for a forest fire of war unpredictable in extent, I am presuming to point out certain trails which can be made into highroads of hope.

One of these trails is that toward health. Recently on the same day there came to the treasurer of the Rockefeller Foundation two items. One was a check for $74,000 to be signed in part payment of a million dollars promised to Japan for the founding of an Institute of Public Health in Tokyo. The other was a news item that Nankai University, a Chinese institution to which the Foundation had given $200,000, had been completely destroyed by Japanese bombs. But the news of the Japanese bombing did not stop the treasurer from signing the check for the Japanese health service. The significance of such a deed is hard to overestimate.

International health work goes on amid the acts and threats of war. Despite our tension with Japan, if a Tokyo earthquake were to recur tomorrow, the American Red Cross would open its purse and the American people would pour out their sympathy to the suffering.

This road, traveled by the health bringers, can become one of the highways of hope through our present wilderness of hate.

When we look at this trail of health we see how it has been widened since Hippocrates brought the medical school at Cos to such a high reputation that he has been called the "father of medicine." In the oath attributed to him and still administered to medical students are to be found the highest ethical principles of private practice. From fifth century Greece to our day the art of healing has had a code of honor second to no other profession. Nevertheless the road to health was restricted to the fortunate few until it was widened under the influence of the Great Physician. Jesus put a missionary passion into the healing art. Deep indeed was the contrast between him who said, "Suffer the little children to come unto me," [2] and Epictetus who querulously asked how he who has to teach mankind can go "looking for something to heat the water in for the baby's bath." [3]

Eighteen centuries were to elapse before the followers of the Nazarene Physician took seriously his challenge to carry their healing work into all the world. Then the hospitals of Edinburgh and London, of New York and Philadelphia began to send their skilled graduates to relieve the suffering of India and China. Sanitation and surgery spread along the Ganges and the Yangtze. Nursing was lifted to the status of a dignified profession. Public health programs caught the popular imagination

[2] Mark 10: 14.
[3] Epictetus, Diatr. 3: 22.

and enlisted community support. Such hideous plagues as tuberculosis and typhoid were driven from their lairs. The science of healing became veritably romantic in its achievements, heroically tracking germs to earth's remotest corners, demonstrating a spirit of service and purity of purpose which could lift the imagination of a Sinclair Lewis from the doldrums of "Main Street" to the enthusiasm of "Arrowsmith," and could make "An American Doctor's Odyssey" a tonic best-seller in a time of disillusioning depression.

Yet in this widening of the road to health, much work has been left for our generation. With all our boasted medical progress healing facilities are still far from being democratically distributed. In the competition and commercialization of medical practice, the doctor is often left to play the rôle of Robin Hood, taking from the rich to help the poor, with the result that the self-respecting middle class suffers neglect. While it is very well for the defenders of the present system to talk about preserving the fine relationship between physician and patient, it should be remembered that over half our American population are without adequate medical or dental attention. Will the medical profession prosecute the self-examination already begun to cure the inequities of private practice and broaden the scope of its service? Apparent, of course, are the dangers of socialized medicine. Personal attention and individual initiative are nowhere more imperative than in the treatment of disease. But the hunger for health, as now aroused, will not be appeased until charity is supplemented and safeguarded by justice. Some form of more efficient practice must replace the random individualistic methods of today.

If the healing profession can purge itself of its inequities, it holds a most—perhaps the most—strategic place in leading society toward the good life. The healers have a hold on the popular interest and affections far stronger than that of preachers or politicians. They can indoctrinate the people with health values, both of body and mind. They can enlist men in those crusades for preserving life which provide a moral equivalent for war. They, with our help, can spread the humane spirit, of which Charles A. Beard says: "It is the humane spirit that points the way to the good life. To reiterate the maxims of this spirit, to restate them in terms of new times, to spread them through education and daily intercourse, to exemplify them in private conduct, to incorporate them in public practice, to cling to them despite our infirmities and hypocrisies—this too is a task of all who fain would make government by the people and for the people endure upon the earth." [4]

A second trail which gives promise of being widened into a highway of hope is that of beauty. In "Lost Horizon," James Hilton expressed the fear that western civilizations might carry their suicidal wars to the point of destroying all their works of art. That is a very real fear in a day when bombs are no respecters of babies or cathedrals. But the love of beauty survives amid the butchery. Embattled Spain smuggled some of her finest canvases to safety outside the danger zone. France is utilizing well-laid plans for the protection of the Louvre's treasures. And Mr. Hilton himself has depicted

[4] Reported in *New York Times*, August 16, 1939.

in his immortal "Goodbye, Mr. Chips" how beauty of character can survive the slaughter of war. Our world may be dark with fears and ugly with disfigurations, but artists still paint and poets still sing.

Moreover, we have now the means of sharing beauty with the many. The best music may be broadcast to the humblest homes. Unsightly slums are giving way to graceful housing. Garden clubs are carrying the gospel of beautification to the smallest hamlet. Public schools are putting increased emphasis on the fine arts. The appreciation of artistic handicraft is growing amid the surfeit of factory-made articles. The craving for culture, however misguided in its direction and eccentric its taste, is one of the most heartening phenomena of our time.

We Americans are no longer content to take our art in tourist doses at European centers. Our young artists are finding the æsthetic climate of Pittsburgh and Toledo quite as invigorating as the Latin Quarter or the dictator-censored circles of central Europe. Art is being drawn into the main stream of American history and philosophy. John Dewey, dean of our philosophers, contends that great art cannot be developed merely through the study of classic forms or of old masters housed in museums by predatory collectors. Art must be indigenous and expressive of contemporary human aspirations. In this, Dewey sets the key of the current emphasis. American art is going native and democratic.

Furthermore the æsthetic quest is winning recognition as an integral part of the social quest for the good life. Writes Irwin Edman of Columbia: "The image of a perfect society is not that of æsthetes in a museum but of artists at their work. The function of the arts in civilization at present is largely that of a dilettante escape for the observer, a truant absorption for the artist. In a rationally ordered society all work would have the quality of art, all enjoyment would have the immediate and glamorous character of æsthetic appreciation." [5]

Yet how far can we approximate such an artistic ideal in our factory age? How much of an artist can a man feel himself to be in his work when that consists of throwing red-hot bolts to a steam riveter or pulling a lever, hour after hour, on a soulless machine? And what chance for the æsthetic quest have the migrant workers of Imperial Valley whose best home is a discarded box car? When one thinks of our mountainous Main Streets, our dingy standardized railroad stations, our highways disfigured by signs and stands, our begrimed mining towns, our drab dwellings, he realizes that the work of beautification has scarcely begun. City planning with an eye to traffic and utility has made much progress, but city zoning with an eye to color and beauty is an innovation barely started in Europe and not yet seriously introduced in America. Our objectives are still size, speed, power, rather than beauty.

Nevertheless the trail has been struck. Through the Federal Arts Project, the government recognized its responsibility for the cultivation of æsthetic resources. Our practical age is coming to see the utility of beauty. One day, during the depression, a Detroit business man sat

[5] Edman, Irwin, "Arts and the Man," to be published. Printed by permission of author.

across the table from me in a dining car. He was giving his views of our national distress. He said: "If you will think of this country organized on a factory basis, you will see that we are carrying too large an overhead and have too few in the production department." Thinking of our governmental overhead, I was inclined to agree with him, until he went on to add: "Why, think of the artists, the musicians, the writers, the preachers, the teachers and all the other non-producers." That kind of reasoning has not the standing it once had. The economic "Lords of Creation" have lost much of their prestige. The creators of beauty and joy are coming into their own.

And why not make this road to beauty an avenue of better understanding between nations? Art and music should be above national boundaries. Although European overlords may erect censorships along the lines of racial distinctions, let us keep the channels of appreciation open to the art of all peoples. The hope of peace lies in those international contacts which go over the heads of governments to the hearts of people. If we can enter into the emotional life of other nationals, appreciate their music, share their æsthetic aspirations, we shall be setting in operation forces ultimately far more potent than the fists of the dictators.

A third trail of hope in our present wilderness is that of truth. The darkness of the future has not checked the pursuit of knowledge. However uncertain the opportunities of tomorrow, youth still crowds our colleges in preparation. The fog of social uncertainty has not dimmed the light of the laboratory. Our physical scientists keep on in the search for truth, not deflected by dictators or mobs. Even war, if it should come tomorrow, would not throttle the inventive genius of man.

The pessimism of the present may well recall the doleful prediction made by the United States Commissioner of Labor in 1886. In his report for that year, the commissioner surveyed the condition of the world. He said that all the necessary railroads and canals had been built, a sufficient network of international communications had been established, an adequate merchant marine had been developed. Then he added that society should settle down and enjoy what had been accomplished, because the next fifty years would see no advance comparable to that of the preceding half-century. At the time that prediction was made, Thomas Edison was 39; Henry Ford, 23; Charles P. Steinmetz, 21; Madame Curie, 19; Robert A. Millikan, 18; Orville Wright, 15; Marconi, 12; Einstein, 7; and the Compton brothers had not yet been born. However dark the present outlook, it is safe to predict that tomorrow will more than match this list of trail-blazers.

Yet the hopeful feature about the search for truth today is not its persistence but its humility. What Galsworthy called the "cockeyed cocksureness" of the specialists is noticeable by its absence. The realms of science are pervaded with a sense of inadequacy. Thoughtful man does not feel himself adequate to confront the world without higher help, and also he does not feel this world in itself adequate for his highest development. One of the paradoxes of our time is that we have more power at our disposal than ever before and yet we seem more powerless. Despite the mechanical slaves which do our bidding, we feel helplessly at the mercy of our machines. Despite the improvements of social organization, men at this moment are being moved like pawns in the hands of war-making governments.

In such a matrix is being born a new seriousness of search for the meaning and mastery of life. Well do I recall the old college fraternity discussions of religion. In the first flush of their scientific studies students often became disturbed about God. Their childhood pictures of Deity began to look like playhouses unfit for man's estate. And so amid the smoke and upholstery of their club houses, those comfortable young men argued about God. But it is one thing to sit comfortably in a smoke-filled room and discuss, "Where is God"; it is quite another to grope after God amid the dangers of a smoke-filling world of battles. It is one thing to believe in a First Cause: it is another to have a God who is a very present help in time of trouble. A few years ago, during the Fundamentalist-Modernist controversy, a professor in an upstate New York college said to a visiting preacher that he wished the ministers who came to that campus would not all feel obliged to prove the existence of God. He desired that some would show how to make contact with the God that is. To that task preaching has now set itself. We have emerged from the mood of cool scientific dialectic to something akin to the longing of the soldier who just before the zero hour of attack turned to his chaplain and said hotly: "What can you tell me about God—quick?"

The sense of bafflement, the feeling of helplessness,

the inadequacy of cleverness—all these are shifting the search for truth toward a divine focus. It is not time to say that men in the mass are finding God, but they are looking for him as never before in our generation. The cool precincts of polite literature reveal some warmth of religious emotion. In theological seminaries the center of interest has moved from the peripheral subjects of social ethics and psychology to the central theme of theology itself. In mass meetings from Madison Square Garden to Hollywood, the Moral Rearmament Movement reflects the popular mood of a return to old religious slogans. Such meetings may not throw much light on the kind of God to be sought, but they evidence the eagerness of search.

Given this new insistence, the search for truth offers promise of becoming a highway of hope. As Sir George Adam Smith once said, we never test the power of prayer until our prayers look up to God like wounded animals with large round eyes of pain. Thus are men looking for divine help today. The search may not arrive at a widespread religious revival. The church as now constituted may not have the genius nor the consecration to lead the hungry host to the divine board. But the trail has been struck. The time is ripe. And never before in my time were visible so many successors of John the Baptist, voices "crying in the wilderness, Prepare ye the way of the Lord, make his paths straight." [6]

A fourth trail of hope is the soundness and goodness of the common man. However diabolical the methods of the dictators of our day, I still have faith in the rank

[6] Matthew 3: 3.

and file of mankind. Lord Baldwin in his last New York address declared: "Two things have impressed themselves on me as the result of my own experience as a political leader. One is the extraordinary instinct of our people to see clearly and to make up their minds quickly and surely on a critical issue. I have seen it many times. It does not surprise me but it fills me with admiration. It makes a man proud to work for such a people. The second thing is their openness to appeals on the highest grounds. The ordinary man in the main wants to do the right thing, and if the politician doesn't believe that, he is himself one of the greatest obstacles to the successful working of the democratic system." [7]

And what Baldwin discovered in his own country could be duplicated even in other lands if we could see behind the scenes and hear the fireside conversations. Behind the press headlines we should see the figure of Kagawa and his Kingdom of God movement in Japan. We should realize the significance of Martin Niemöller and his faithful congregation in Berlin. We need to learn the lesson which lifted Elijah out of his gloom, namely, that there are hosts who have not bowed the knee to Baal. If there were sneers at Munich, there were also cheers, sincere cheers from peace-desiring people of Germany as well as of Britain.

For me personally the simple goodness of men is a most powerful restorative of my faith in God. I find it easier to account for evil in God's world than to account for goodness in a godless world. A bad man may be explained as a good one gone wrong, but a good man is

[7] Reported in the *New York Times*, August 17, 1939.

somewhat more than an evil one in reverse. Hate may be love turned sour, but love is more than sweetened bitterness. I can understand how God has to give his children freedom of choice for the sake of character development, and how some can turn their liberty into the excesses of a Hitler or a Napoleon, but if there be no love or justice at the heart of the universe, I cannot understand why a man should lay down his life for his friends or why a Christ should pray for his crucifiers. I can explain a hurricane as the orderly winds gone awry, but I cannot account for the rainbow without the sun. Hence the goodness which I see in men strikes me as the reflection of a godliness at the center of things.

And despite the quenched hopes of the last two decades, I feel that the gains of those years are not entirely lost. Men who have looked at large horizons cannot again be content with their old petty provincialisms. The dreams of peace have left a deposit of idealism which even war cannot utterly destroy. Cynics may say that when the drums beat the pacifists will meekly fall into line, but we have no adequate precedent to justify such an assertion, for no previous war was preceded by a peace education paralleling that of the last twenty years. The call to kill will find many pulpit leaders presenting answers rather than arms. And more significant was the hesitation on the part of even dictators to issue the call to kill. Governments held back from war through events which twenty-five years ago would have unleashed its horrors. In this has been registered a gain which war itself cannot erase.

Society may slip back—aye, at some points it has already tragically lapsed. But it does not go all the way back. This is the wine of good hope which John Steinbeck presses from the "Grapes of Wrath." He says: "Man, unlike any other thing organic or inorganic in the universe, grows beyond his work, walks up the stairs of his concepts, emerges ahead of his accomplishments. This you may say of man—when theories change and crash, when schools, philosophies, when narrow dark allies of thought, national, religious, economic, grow and disintegrate, man reaches, stumbles forward, painfully, mistakenly sometimes. Having stepped forward, he may slip back, but only half a step, never the full step back. This you may say and know it and know it. This you may know when the bombs plummet out of the black planes on the marketplace, when prisoners are stuck like pigs, when the crushed bodies drain filthily in the dust. . . . And this you can know—fear the time when Manself will not suffer and die for a concept, for this one quality is the foundation of Manself, and this one quality is man, distinctive in the universe." [8]

Some four or five years ago, a banker, a retired business man and a minister were together at lunch. Into the conversation came the case of a banker who had recently been convicted of irregularities. The elderly steel executive made the remark that when he was active in Wall Street some twenty-five years before, certain of the modern questionable practices were not countenanced. In those earlier days, said he, a man's word was as good as his bond. And he bemoaned the lapsing of personal integrity. In reply, the active young banker coun-

[8] Steinbeck, John, "Grapes of Wrath." Viking Press, pp. 204–205.

tered: "That may all be true, but remember also that there were some things you men of that day took for granted which would not be tolerated today." Both men had a point. There is a growing laxity at some places in personal standards; there is also an increasing awareness of social responsibilities. We do not advance evenly in our ethics. The emphasis of recent years has been on the social rather than the personal conscience. Now without reducing our efforts to widen the road of social advance, the challenge comes to recover for the individual the truth that "strait is the gate, and narrow is the way, which leadeth unto life." [9] The Highway of Hope must also be a Pilgrim's Progress.

[9] Matthew 7: 14.

# Chapter VI

Nov. 29
1940

# THE CHALLENGE OF CHANGE

LIFE may sometimes have long stretches of slow motion like that of a retarded cinema. Then suddenly it is speeded up into a syncopation of crises. Which period puts the severer strain on personality?

There is peril in uneventful living. A plant may flourish best when the processes of growth go on in undisturbed serenity. But it is not so with human life. Even the body of man seems to deteriorate when the current of life flows too smoothly. It would almost appear that we age faster in the placid setting of secluded, sheltered places than amid the hurly-burly of stormy activity. We grow old, not so much through the passing of time as through the repetitions of actions. Hence, when our range of activities and interests contract, and we do the same things over and over, our bodies wear out faster. They settle and sag. On the other hand, emergencies which nearly exhaust our strength seem to open the channels of fresh energy. Our physical welfare is benefited by changes, even by those which at the time seem to tax our endurance.

And the mind, even more than the body, suffers when life is too uneventful. The unstirred mind, like the unused attic, gets cobwebs in its corners. Whole sections of the imagination are neglected. Thought settles into grooves and goes round and round in vicious circles. For this reason the Master of Life repeatedly called the set-

65

tled adults of his day to "become as little children" if they would have the Kingdom of Heaven within themselves. Their stiff and brittle minds needed limbering. A wise old bishop once remarked that every man should change his job between the ages of forty-five and fifty-five. A sudden shift of circumstances will sometimes shake minds up and renew their youthful vitality. A friend of mine now in his late sixties is a marvel of youthfulness. His life would appear almost a series of crises, fortunes made and lost. But jumping from crisis to crisis, he has kept his mind agile. He is always steamed up over some new personal enthusiasm or social emergency. His freshness illustrates the fact that steam, explosive though it be, is better than rust for our mental boilers.

And when there are no changes, our spirits, like our bodies and minds, deteriorate. The sunshine on the surface of a placid stream does not purify the waters. Rapids and falls do that. Likewise the stream of experience needs its times of turbulent quickening.

> One crowded hour of glorious life
> Is worth an age without a name.[1]

Our emotions become shallow and stagnant unless we have some experiences which stir us to the depths of our beings. The cultivation of calm and quietude, although much needed, can be carried too far. A bishop once wrote, to the rector of a rural parish, that he was planning to visit him soon and was looking forward to a quiet Sunday in his country church. The minister wrote back: "My parish doesn't need a quiet Sunday; it needs an

[1] Scott, Sir Walter, "Answer."

earthquake." There are times when we need earthquake experiences which crack the crust of convention, shatter our flimsy complacencies and shake our plans to their foundations. The Psalmist was voicing this truth when he wrote: "Because they have no changes, therefore they fear not God." [2]

In view of this peril of uneventful living, we should thank God that he has matched us with this hour. Our time has all the challenge of change. Whitehead of Harvard puts it none too strongly when he writes: "Mankind is now in one of its rare moods of shifting its outlook. The mere compulsion of tradition has lost its force. Either we must succeed in providing a rational coördination of impulses and thoughts or for centuries civilization will sink into a welter of minor excitements. We must produce a great age or see the collapse of the upward striving of our race."

Such is the challenge of our day. Will this time, so pregnant with crisis, bring forth a "great age" or a "welter of minor excitements"? The social issue is the personal problem enlarged. Can we so handle the changes of fortune that we "get the breaks" or do we allow the breaks to get us?

For one thing, the very interruptions of life's regularity can serve to show us the continuity of the current. A little over a century ago, a young American was returning from a sojourn in England. He had a bent for science and had been interested in the study of electromagnetism. In his mind there lingered a sentence which he had memorized in his scientific studies. This was the

[2] Psalm 55: 19.

sentence: "If the circuit of electricity be interrupted, the fluid will become visible; and when it passes, it will leave an impression upon any intermediate body." As the young man pondered that idea, the query arose whether it might not be possible to turn those flashes of visibility into a code of signals for transmitting messages. Out of that inspiration, the young traveler, whose name was Samuel Finley Breese Morse, invented the telegraph. This principle of electricity has its parallel in the life of the spirit. There is a Morse code of the soul whereby the interruptions of life's current can give the flash which illumines the routine of living.

A break in the family circle, for instance, brings its pang of loneliness, but it may also serve to remind us, as it did Carlyle, of the love which flowed so steadily through the household that it was taken for granted without gratitude. A break in business brings hardship, but it may also throw fresh light on the favorable factors which continue and may raise the question of making a living into the higher issue of making a life. A break in health takes the patient out of the stream of activity, but thereby it may show him what the real current of life is as distinguished from its eddies. Thus an interruption may reveal the continuity.

One of the secrets of victorious living is to see through a wife's momentary flash of anger to her enduring love, to glimpse through the treachery of a false friend the fidelity of countless others. Carry this habit a bit further. Think of the things happening to one individual: he goes to school, breaks an arm, enlists in a war, is shell-shocked, has a brain tumor removed, practices law, is

elected to Congress, and amid all these changes his bodily parts are being replaced in seven-year cycles. Yet
amid all these shifts, the identity of the self continues.
And by the way, this ability of personality to survive
earthly change lends further credence in my own thinking to the real possibility of living through the dissolu-
tion incident to physical death.

It is quite as important to see the continuity beneath
the good breaks as beneath the bad. Robert Blatchford,
the British publicist, was once asked to what he attributed
his success. He replied, "Luck." In explanation, he said
that the two most decisive turns in his life seemed due to
chance. His mother, an actress, was faced with a choice
of residence at one point in her career. Not knowing
which city to choose she left the selection to her two
young sons, who made the decision without any logical
reasoning. In the city to which they thus happened to
go, Blatchford eventually met his wife. And then his
business opening came through his acquaintance with a
man whom he met apparently by chance in a rooming
house. Thus, in the two very important matters of his
marriage and his work, Blatchford seemed to have been
the beneficiary of luck. Such testimonies might be multiplied until in the words of Ecclesiastes we could say,
"Time and chance happeneth to them all." [3] Events do
occur by no traceable law. But there is a wide difference
between the gambling attitude which counts on the
breaks and the scientific planning which allows for them.
The former leads to will-o'-the-wisp logic and fly-by-
night following of best bets; the latter leads to firmness

[3] Ecclesiastes 9: 11.

of principle combined with flexibility of expectation. The farmer, like the gambler, takes his chances, but out of them he evolves ever better ways of mastering the hazards of weather. He counts on the laws which underlie the breaks of luck.

Similarly, in our social outlook, do we see the tangled events of our troubled time as a "tale told by an idiot," or can we trace the clues of any larger meaning? In a book of fiction written during the early post-war days, Hamilton Gibbs made one of his characters describe the European leaders as blindfolded camels turning an Egyptian waterwheel, thinking in their blindness that they were going great distances but in reality going nowhere. So seem the vicious circles of political action. Yet Thomas Mann, with every personal reason to be cynical, sees a different interpretation. Out of his brooding time-sense, so profound in its depth, comes this conviction: "Outwardly we live in an epoch of retrograde civilization, wherein treaties are worthless, lawlessness and disloyalty are the contagious mode. But there is an inward spirit among men which has entered upon a new moral epoch; one of simplification, of humble-minded recognition of the difference between good and evil. This is its way of returning to the primitive and renewing its youth." [4] The interpreter of "Joseph in Egypt" can thus trace a pattern through the breaks which have befallen the sons of Joseph in our day.

The breaks may serve not only to show us the continuity of life's currents but also to spiritualize them.

[4] *Survey Graphic*, February, 1939, p. 151.

The tendency of undisturbed living is toward materialistic attitudes. Our physical concerns are ever to the fore.
Our five senses keep us occupied with the securing of
their satisfactions. Left to itself, life gravitates toward
the bodily interests.

Alexis Carrel brings the charge against America that
our people have been engrossed in the development of
our material resources to the neglect of our inner po-
tencies, thus leaving "Man the Unknown." Most of us
have to confess that we find it easier to take up ready-to-
hand material interests than to push back into the spiritual. "Things are in the saddle and ride mankind," until
something halts them. We come to measure social progress by mechanical inventions and civilization by bodily
comforts. An American traveler, lost three days in the
jungles of India, finally came across a missionary com-
pound, whereupon he entered in his journal, "After those
jungle nights, it was good to sleep again in a Christian
bed." Is that what distinguishes our Christian civilization
—Christian beds, Christian refrigerators, Christian ele-
vators?

To be sure, the most secular-minded do at times feel
the surge of the spiritual. One such hour is that of marriage. A young couple may have little or no concern for
the regular services of religion, but when they arrive
at the high moment of linking life with life, they wish
to come before an altar. In this persistent desire there is
something more than force of custom and respectability.
When the destinies of two individuals are being joined,
there is more at stake than a civil contract or a property

adjustment. It is a union of spirit with spirit, and at such a moment even the most materially-minded feel drawn toward the Divine Spirit.

Another hour wherein we human beings feel the nearness of God is that in which a child is born to us. A man and wife may deem themselves so competent to handle their own lives without divine help that they never give thought to the church. But the coming of a child gives a new responsibility and a new sense of need. Personally, I know few more soul-lifting sights than that of proud young parents humbly and joyously dedicating their child to God and asking divine aid in its rearing.

Along with marriage and birth, there is a third turn in life's routine when the spiritual tends to break through the material. That is the hour of death. The wider my experience, the more I am impressed with the dignity of human nature in the presence of death. The coarsest natures take on a certain nobility when they stand beside a grave. It is not merely that they reach out for divine help, but the divine in them seems to come out to help others. The kindness and consideration which death calls forth bring a certain halo to the crudest environments. When in the presence of such sorrow, we open the Twenty-third Psalm and are led beside the "still waters" and green pastures, it is not hard to feel the nearness of the Good Shepherd. Or when we turn to the fourteenth chapter of John's Gospel, and hear, "In my Father's house are many mansions," life seems to open into a vastness far transcending the world of time and space. A devoted daughter, after her father's funeral service, expressed her faith thus: "Every time the door swings to let a loved one through from the visible to the invisible, I feel more confidence in the divine care."

In addition to these high moments of birth, marriage and death, other experiences come which cause us to "grope around the wall of life in search of the crevices through which God may be seen." But mere change, however drastic, does not necessarily make men spiritual. Loss of health does not always turn men to God. Sometimes it only makes them more fretfully concerned with their physical condition. Likewise loss of property does not always lead men to higher spiritual attitudes. It is possible to be as materialistic with a little money as with a lot. In this fact we see why the business depression has not begotten a religious revival. Our eyes have been riveted as closely on the almighty dollar during the depressed '30s, as during the booming '20s. Nor do the dangers of our present time assure a popular return to religion. The threat of war may make us afraid without making us spiritual.

Like Franklin with his kite and key, we may catch the secret of the higher power in the lightning flash of a storm, but the flash must be translated into power for daily living. How wasteful to leave our spiritual contacts unused except in rare moments of insight. It is as if we used our telephones only to call the fire department and our radios only to send S O S signals. That which becomes luminous in the crisis can become "the light of all our being."

These elusive moments of divine insight may be translated into a sustaining radiance by cultivation. Muriel Lester, through more than thirty years of settlement work in one of the drabbest parts of London, has developed a formula for keeping the lustre when the breaks are with her or against her. This is her schedule of spiritual cultivation:

"When you wake in the morning, immediately greet God as an objective reality . . . an Unseen Presence close beside you. Picture him as radiant beauty, creative power, unfailing serenity and love. Before you come down to breakfast, make a prayer dedicating your entire day to God and His service. . . . At each meal during the day thank God for his mercy in providing food for you, and then make a prayer for those who must go hungry. . . . As you go about your work throughout the day, remember that all the individuals whom you meet belong to God just as you do. . . . At the end of the day, in a moment of silence and in the conscious presence of God, let the failures and anxieties of the day pass through your mind and then vanish forever. As they vanish, God will lift the burden from your spirit, will make everything begin to seem clear again. When you finally drop to sleep let your last thought be this . . . 'Father, into thy hands I commend my spirit.' " [5] A spirit strengthened by such practices is prepared for the worst the bad breaks can bring, and for the best the good breaks can give.

Some are lifted from their personal crises by commitment to new causes, as in the case of John Bright who turned from the tragedy of his wife's death to lead the movement for repealing the Corn Laws of England. Others learn from the breaks in fortune a new resigna-

[5] *Federal Council Bulletin,* December, 1936.

tion to the inevitable, as witness the diary of Henri Amiel after he had learned of his incurable malady: "On waking it seemed to me that I was staring into the future with startled eyes. . . . Health cut off means marriage, travel, study and work, forbidden or endangered. It means life reduced by five-sixths. . . . Thy will be done." That last sentence reveals the victory.

Or try to imagine what fortified the spirit of Abraham Lincoln against the lightning crises which crashed about his head during his later years. As Robert Sherwood unfolds the character of his hero in "Abe Lincoln in Illinois," one feature particularly impressed me. The loss of Anne Rutledge left the young Lincoln seemingly burned out. The power of the lethargic giant appeared to have been short-circuited. And then the drama brings the current of energy back to Lincoln's spirit through the near-tragedy of a friend's child. Called upon to pray in that family crisis, the long gaunt figure seemed to connect with a Higher Power, and through him began to throb a passion for a whole people. Why did the earlier sorrow exhaust Lincoln and the later one energize him? The only explanation whereby I can link the two scenes is that during the intervening years the brooding spirit of the man had acquired what Stephen Vincent Benét reveals in the lines he puts on the lips of Lincoln:

O Will of God
I am a patient man, and I can wait
Like an old gun flint buried in the ground
While the slow years pile up like smoldering leaves
Above me, underneath the rake of Time. . . .
That is my only virtue as I see it,

Ability to wait and hold my own
And keep my own resolves once they are made.
In spite of what the smarter people say
I can't be smart the way that they are smart,
I've known that since I was an ugly child,
It teaches you—to be an ugly child,
It teaches you—to lose a thing you love.[6]

Such are some of the ways by which men have come through the challenge of change "more than conquerors."

[6] Benét, Stephen Vincent, "John Brown's Body." Doubleday Doran, p. 214.

# Chapter VII

Nov. 29

# THE MAGIC OF COURAGE

1940

THE power of encouragement is a quality even greater than the possession of courage. A man may demonstrate his own bravery in a way that makes others feel their own weakness and fear. A parachute jumper, for instance, by his daring feat manifests his own personal courage, but he does not inspire me with a boldness to go and do likewise, whereas on one or two occasions the quiet confidence of an airplane stewardess has restored my spirits when the plunging of the plane had shaken my nerve. Some individuals may be personally bold enough to be star performers and yet make others more conscious of the surrounding darkness. Stars with all their brilliance do not help violets to lift their drooping heads.

Our day does not greatly need star performers of reckless daring, but we do need most desperately those who impart courage to others. Ours is a time when fear has reached almost to the proportions of hysteria. The road ahead in business lies somewhat in a fog. The integrity of our American institutions is threatened by subversive movements. The war now raging in Europe will be little short of miraculous if it avoids us. This has been called the Explosive Century, marked by the upsurging of the unpredictable. This is a time of crisis involving our livelihood, even our lives. It is cruel as well as futile to cry peace, peace, when there is no peace.

Yet just because the day is so hot with danger, we

need to keep cool. In perilous places the courageous person keeps the surest footing, while the one who gets frightened and flustered does the foolish and reckless thing. On the highway the driver who becomes scared loses control and invites accident. In the heat of anger, fear often makes a man strike first. It is fear rather than bravery which starts war. Scared persons are the prey of the demagogue in politics, the quack in medicine, and the war-monger among nations. When people lose their heads, they are most likely to lose their lives.

Hence courage gives not only a sense of security, but the fact of it as well. The brave person turns his face rather than his back toward danger, thereby seeing the perils for what they are, no more and no less. Thus he is prepared to meet them with open eyes. And thus also he curbs the fear which comes to the fleeing man who sees the dangers over his shoulder for, as William James said, "We are afraid because we run, rather than run because we are afraid."

The will to be brave has a magic power to arouse energy and release unexpected resources. This is the truth the Master told so picturesquely in his parable of the talents, ending with the enigmatic assertion, "Unto everyone that hath shall be given, and he shall have abundance; but from him that hath not shall be taken away even that which he hath." [1] The negative souls who bury their talents in napkins lose them. The timid persons who make a habit of playing safe find the safety zones of life getting smaller and smaller, and their stake in the world becoming less and less. The fearful spirit lives by the law

[1] Matthew 25: 29.

of subtraction, his energy ebbs away, his valor declines, his faith shrinks. On the other hand the man with a courageous will-to-believe lives by a law of addition, confidence begetting confidence, "tribulation working patience; patience, experience; and experience, hope."

To use Thomas Carlyle's trenchant expression, the basic question to be answered by each one for himself is, *"Wilt thou be a hero or a coward?"* The hero within us does not wait until he can see through a situation beyond the shadow of a doubt. He starts while the shadows of doubt are thick upon him. With the lantern of faith illuminating the next step and then the next, he launches out into the darkness. This will to be brave can accomplish wonders by the sheer force of its own strength. The magic of courage can restore one's own morale and hearten the spirits of others, as "Stonewall" Jackson put heart into his comrades by holding his ground or as Phil Sheridan rallied his retreating troops when he dashed down the Virginia turnpike, shouting, "Turn, boys, turn, we're going back." (I believe that is not quite all Sheridan said, but anyhow he turned the tide from defeat to victory.)

Nevertheless, our times need something more than a natural hopefulness or an invincible good humor or the will to be brave. The delightful little books on optimism which pour from the press no doubt help many to "brighten the corner where they are." But little private compartments of sweetness and light, good as they may be, are not adequate for a world as dark and bitter as ours. And many of the Pollyanna optimists that come buzzing around me remind me of the fireflies on a summer night which reveal their own glow but do not give enough light to read by.

A courage contagious enough for our day must be able to give a reason for the faith that is in it. We are not schoolboys who can be rallied merely by bright slogans and hearty slaps on the back. For a time we may prime the pumps of our spirits by self-stimulation. For an occasional fainting spell a dash of cold water may be sufficient to revive the patient. But pernicious anemia is not to be cured by repeated dashes of cold water; the blood stream must be built up. Our day calls for transfusion of courage from sources deeper than ourselves.

Dean Willard Sperry, describing recently the changes of thought which he had experienced during the last decade or two, said that he was reminded of his boyhood along the Maine coast. As a lad he was allowed to row his little dory around the sheltered bay. Occasionally he would pluck up courage and row past the sheltering points of the tiny inlet. Out in the open ocean he could feel the swell and roll of the deep sea. So, said the dean, the events of the past two decades have carried us out of the quiet bays into the deep waters.

And truly they have. Every adult is inclined to look back to his childhood, if normal, as a comparatively quiet harbor sheltered behind the protecting presence of parents. The leaving of home is a launching out into the deep. Yet while this is true in normal times, we have been living through abnormal years. Young people coming to maturity during the last decade have set sail into a world where the storm is on and where multitudes are completely at sea, in the sense that they have lost both their moorings and their bearings. The old shore lines are lost to view. The old moral landmarks are hidden in fog.

Twenty-five years ago our land seemed safely sheltered behind two oceans. We had begun to enjoy world trade but we had not begun to worry about world responsibilities. As Professor Frederick Grant has said: "America was like some rural family which has grown unbelievably opulent, then moves to town, and while enjoying the wealth, ease and diversions of city life, is unwilling at first to assume any of the responsibilities the new residence entails." [2] We Americans felt pretty secure from foreign entanglements because England stood like a shepherd herding the European nations safely eastward away from us. But now we are not so sure Britain will or can continue to shepherd the unruly nations.

In the moral and religious realms also, we have been carried out into the conflict with great new evils. In my boyhood we heard many sermons on personal sins like lust and greed and drunkenness, but very few on the sins of war and race hatred, and none that I recall on the sin of worshiping the state. Now we "wrestle not against flesh and blood" so much as "against principalities and powers." As boys we heard of paganism but we thought of it as existing mainly in what we called heathen lands where the Christian gospel had not yet penetrated. We talked about the heathen Chinese and on our missionary maps the great dark continent was Africa. But no longer do we locate paganism away off yonder in non-

[2] Grant, Frederick, "Frontiers of Christian Thinking." Willett, Clark and Company, p. 139.

Christian countries, for we are deluged with pagan elements in our own communities. Truly, as the prophet said to ancient Tyre, so it might be said to modern America, "Thy rowers have brought thee into great waters." [3]

The courage adequate for tomorrow must be one capable of carrying us through deep waters. Such courage requires, for one thing, a faith able to sustain us when we are beyond our depth. When a person can no longer touch bottom, it is not enough to say, "Straighten up and be a man." Mere strength on one's own part, the mere will to be brave, is not sufficient. In fact there is often need of relaxing one's strain. When the inexperienced swimmer is tossed into the water, he tries to support himself by his own frantic efforts. He beats about furiously with his hands and feet as if everything depended on his own energy. But the graceful, trained swimmer combines the movements of his body with the buoyancy of the water. So in the deep waters of life, we must learn to supplement our efforts with reliance on a divine support.

Sometimes we discover this divine aid in a decisive time of testing. Justin Wroe Nixon recounts the revelation which came to him, when in a crucial decision he risked much for the sake of an ideal. He writes: "The experience was like that of a man sinking in a bog and coming unexpectedly on firm ground. . . . Out of the experience emerged this bit of wisdom, that when a man rests his all on the Best he knows, he discovers that the ideal thing which seemed so fragile when he stepped out upon

[3] Ezekiel 27: 26.

it has foundations which make it the most utterly real Supporting Power he has found in life." [4]

Or it may be that we find this supplementing strength at the extremity of our own exertion. When a person pursues his duty until, as he says, he is "at the end of his string," and then keeps on, he begins to release power he did not know he had. He comes out of a long and trying experience saying, "If I had known in advance what I had to endure, I could not have stood it;" but in the ordeal he discovered the truth that "as thy days so shall thy strength be." When we have done our best and still hold on, there comes One "able to do exceeding abundantly above all that we ask or think, according to the power that worketh in us."

Or, we may catch this courage-sustaining faith through contact with heroic spirits. There is a contagion of health and confidence just as truly as of disease and fear. Even the printed page can transmit the germs of courageous faith. So much of our daily reading is enervating. The news of crime and disasters and diplomacy tend to lessen our moral confidence. The current views of our general situation lead to the conclusion that physical force rules the day. Dictators try to bluff the democracies by brandishing their mailed fists. Blustering men with strong hands and heavy purses seem to dominate the circles wherein we live. But when we survey the long stretch of time, we see that it is "not by might nor by power but by my spirit, saith the Lord of Hosts." The Masters of the spirit outlast the so-called strong men.

[4] Nixon, Justin Wroe, "An Emerging Christian Faith." Harper & Bros., p. 150.

The generals who led the troops in the Trojan war are forgotten, but Homer still lives in the hearts of those who love beauty. Cleon, the powerful political and military leader of fifth century Athens, is buried in the dust of oblivion, but Socrates who served as a private in Cleon's army still lives because he gave himself to the service of truth. Augustus Caesar plays no part in today's affairs, but a carpenter's son, born in one of Caesar's provinces, is still the most potent personality in the world, because he manifested a power of the spirit which even the tomb could not hold.

When we thus put ourselves in the company of luminous and heroic spirits and then survey the long panoramas of history, we find our pulse quicken and our eyes brighten. And our courage needs to be built up by more hero worship and devotional reading. America at the moment is witnessing an awakening of the heroic note in literature and drama. From the era of Dreiser with his profound pity and Lewis with his pervasive satire, we are turning to a glorification of all things American. Let us hope we are emerging from the mood described sarcastically by Dorothy Canfield: "In this our little period of history, filled with hate and scorn and fear and restlessness as it is, most of the well-written books are naturally those which express hate and fear, scorn and recklessness. To be bitterly, sickly, helplessly dissatisfied with your life wherever it is laid, is the fashion now. . . . To conceive of human life as a sordid trap into which inexorable instincts betray helpless men and women to their doom is a convention of our time." [5]

[5] Canfield, Dorothy, in *Book of the Month Club Bulletin*, May, 1933.

It is high time to strike a new note, to cultivate the kind of reading which puts courage into our people, provided we safeguard the new trend of Americana from sentimentalism and uncritical nationalism, from paralleling the evils of Germany's Nordic myth, from mistaking bigness for greatness, from confusing spiritual bravery with physical bluster.

Courage adequate for tomorrow needs to be sustained also by a sense of social solidarity. A swimmer, however good, cannot survive long on the high seas. Even a rowboat, however sturdy, is of limited help when the sea billows roll. My personal feeling about our present social situation is somewhat like that which I have experienced walking the deck of an ocean liner on a dark and stormy night. As I have looked over the rail at the ominous murky waters, I have shuddered at the thought of being pitched out alone into the deep. And then how warming and cheering it was to walk back into the fellowship of the lighted salon. Similarly I feel the need of touching shoulders with like-minded spirits in these stormy times.

Ours is a day when the seekers after righteousness need a sense of comradeship as almost never before. To think that we can check the organized forces of godlessness by mere individualistic piety is as futile as to try to irrigate the Sahara with an atomizer. Of course, each of us should be interested in his own salvation, but Jesus never taught that the way of salvation was to let the world go to the devil while we sought sweetness and light for ourselves. Of course, we need personal regeneration, but if each householder had a well of pure water in his own backyard, would that give a water supply adequate to protect the town from fires or even to clean the streets? No, we need social action to make our individual courage and goodness effective.

A visitor from France called recently to see several Americans. He had two objectives in coming to America at this time. One, he feels that a proper handling of the refugee problem requires an organization as universal as the Red Cross, for no piecemeal or spasmodic efforts will be able to care for the refugees that he sees increasing in the next few years, even in his own country. He also is hoping to see the democratic nations develop some kind of patriotic ritual which will fire and fuse the free peoples as the Nazi and Fascist ceremonies and symbolism have stirred the citizens of dictator lands. Hitler and Mussolini know and use the psychology of solidarity. As the great gatherings at Nuremberg reinforce the courage and enthusiasm of the individual Nazi, let us devise demonstrations to strengthen the individual within democracy.

And let Christendom multiply the manifestations of unity on a scale larger than national. Only the long future can measure the value of the Oxford Conference of 1937, held at a time when the governments were barricading themselves behind new breastworks of hate. That conference revealed how many there are dwelling under different flags and yet clinging to the same cross of Christ. Those who attended it came back with courage renewed as did Elijah when he found how many had not bowed the knee to Baal. It is too dark and dangerous a time for the individual to keep up his courage indefinitely doing picket duty. The seekers after righteousness need to cheer one another on.

Yet to keep up courage for tomorrow we must have more than cheering comradeship. This must be supplemented by a fortifying purpose. Familiar in personal living is the quickening power of a purpose. A woman in a New York hospital was recently lying despondent. The doctors had done everything needful from the medical standpoint. Organically she was all right. But her trouble lay in the fact that she had lived a very active life with an infirm husband and several grandchildren dependent on her, and then suddenly these responsibilities had been removed. What she needed to revive her spirits was a new interest in life, something to live for.

What is true of the individual is also true on the large national scale. A nation to be strong must live for big ends. Dean Gauss of Princeton has pointed out an illuminating feature of Rome's fall. We commonly say that the Roman Empire fell under the invasion of the Vandal hordes. But how large was the invading host? The dean asserts there were only about eighty thousand altogether, which meant a fighting force of perhaps not more than twenty thousand. What would an enemy of twenty thousand have meant back in the rugged days of the republic? Why Julius Caesar would probably have disposed of such a danger in a few days' fighting. But in the effete empire of the fifth century, the Roman people no longer saw anything in their system for which they greatly cared to live or for which they greatly cared to die. The Roman Empire no longer had purposes big enough to call forth the greatness of its citizens.

Need we sharpen the point to prick the conscience of America and the other democracies today? Russia, Germany and Italy have fortified their people with purposes which appear to them worth working and fighting for. We deplore their dangerous methods and their curtailment of individual rights. But denunciation is not enough. We must match those countries by giving our people causes big enough to call out our courage and devotion in some comparable degree.

Yes, we must do better than those dictator-ridden lands. Their objectives are not good enough to keep up courage indefinitely. I do not believe that Hitler with his Nordic myth can hold his followers in a long, sacrificial war. He cannot keep up the spirit of sacrifice since he has taken out the religion of the cross. It takes a God who sacrifices to keep men sacrificing.

The half-gods of the state are not good enough to see us through as nations. The will to be brave is not enough for us as individuals. Only when our courage is undergirded by faith in a God who guarantees the triumph of spiritual values and our hearts are fired with his enduring purposes—only then have we something big enough to live for. Then we are brave enough to live for tomorrow.

# Chapter VIII

Du. 6 '40

# THE LIMITS OF LOVE

LOVE is an overworked word for an unemployed emotion. Why not give the term a rest? No doubt many will do so for the duration of the war as they did twenty years ago. But then after the blood-letting is over, the words brotherly love will undoubtedly come pouring forth again, dripping from diplomats and gushing from pulpits. Our speech has been profaned by the vain use of the word, love, even more than by the vain taking of the Lord's name. Can we stop this profanation of our most sacred common noun?

Love is the identifying mark of a Christian. Whatever else he may have, that he must have. "By this shall all men know that ye are my disciples, if ye have love one to another." [1] And yet despite the centrality of this command, we do not treat it with the strictness accorded the Ten Commandments. If we break the old command, "Thou shalt not steal," we are punished by the laws of the state. If we violate the commandment, "Thou shalt not commit adultery," we are put beyond the pale of decency. If we commit murder by transgressing the law, "Thou shalt not kill," we may even be put to death.

But if we break the commandment, "Love one another," what happens to us? Does society step in to punish us? At times it is quite the opposite. While the World War was on, if an American had openly admitted that he

[1] John 13: 35.

loved the Germans, he would have been ostracized socially if not interned physically. Fifteen years ago during the vogue of the Ku Klux Klan, some men were elected to public office because they boasted of their hatred for Negroes, for Jews, for foreigners. And in our day some gain a leadership in politics and even in the church because they are such eloquent denouncers and venomous haters. Instead of punishing men for breaking the commandment, "Love one another," we often promote them.

Perhaps our lax attitude toward this commandment may be due to its indefiniteness. The vivid old laws of the Decalogue are mostly in the negative, and a negative commandment is definite like a red light on the highway. When the light flashes red, the car stops, whether it be a Rolls Royce or a Ford. But when a green light gives the signal to go ahead, we obey it at different speeds, some at thirty, some at fifty, some at seventy miles per hour. Similarly the command to love one another, being a signal to go ahead, we obey it at such differing speeds. A Saint Francis goes forward with a love for the outcast and the leper which so far outdistances our little personal affections that we abandon the hope of keeping up with him. And a Jesus of Nazareth demonstrates a love for his enemies which to us seems impossible of approximation. We are disposed to say, "If that is the kind of love it takes to be a Christian, it is beyond us." Hence we cease to take the commandment of love as a strict measurement, and leave it as a kind of pious wish.

Thus we are allowing our ethics of love to mush down into a standardless sentimentalism. At a good-will forum of Roman Catholics, Protestants and Jews, a well-intentioned woman asked, "Does not the whole question simmer down into preaching the Fatherhood of God and the Brotherhood of man?" Ah, yes, but those big broad generalizations have just about as much force in the popular mind as do the high-sounding phrases incorporated in the planks of a political platform. Such weak wishful thinking has resulted in the condition described by the boy in the geography class to which the teacher put the question, "What is the shape of the earth?" The little fellow replied, "Father says it is in about the worst shape it's ever been." In a world which the means of travel and communication are transforming into a neighborhood, men are becoming less neighborly. To be delivered from the vagueness of mere good intentions, let us either be definite in our doing of good or drop the pious language.

May we test the limits of love by a few simple measurements, following the figure of the four dimensions which the Apostle Paul desired for his disciples when he craved that they might know "the breadth and length and depth and height" of Christian love.

First, the *breadth* of our brotherly feelings. The minimum requirement of a decent human being is that he shall love those who love him. The person who does not respond to the affection shown toward him is something less than normal. Nevertheless, it might be revealing to rummage among our recollections. We might discover how many channels of love within our intimate circles have been allowed to dry up. And it might be worth while to ask whether the tendency of modern living is not toward widening our acquaintances and narrowing our real friendships. Cynical, even brutal, sounds the assertion of a well-known writer that he had many friends but not more than a dozen the news of whose death would spoil his appetite for breakfast. But among our so-called friends, how many have we who could break our hearts by what happens to them?

And when we lift the test from our intimate circles to the larger social relations, how brotherly are we? During the Great War, Gilbert Murray said that he went around the quadrangles of Oxford with a heavy heart because he could not throw off the thought of the fine young fellows who were dying for him in France. While these lines are being written, despairing men are taking their own lives in Danzig, refugees have been roaming the seas looking for a haven, and only God knows what is happening in China. How much do we in America care? Is Aldous Huxley correct in asserting that the radio, the cinema and the press have made us so repeatedly aware of others' sufferings that we have grown callous to them? It would seem so. Oh, to be sure, on the fateful first of September the outbreak of hostilities on the Polish border was such startling news that radio reports were incessant, pedestrians on the sidewalks of New York looked a bit dazed and the air was electric with emotional intensity. But if the war should continue for months as a mere European conflict, will the casualty reports remain headline news or will we Americans weary of the war campaigns as we have wearied of the peace programs?

Has the widening of our horizons been accompanied by a narrowing of our sympathies? Consider these figures displayed recently at the National Stewardship Conference in Chicago. For the years 1932 to 1937 we Americans increased our expenditures for jewelry twenty-four per cent, for theaters forty-one per cent, for tobacco forty-three per cent, for automobiles one hundred and eighty-eight per cent, for whiskey one hundred per cent, for radio sets two hundred and twenty per cent, and for beer over six hundred per cent. During the same period we decreased our giving to churches nineteen per cent, to church benevolences twenty-eight per cent, and to community chests, including hospitals, twenty-two per cent. Without discussing the worth of some of the items for which our money went, the fact stands out with stark clarity that during recent years we in America have been vastly increasing the amounts spent on ourselves while tragically decreasing our gifts to others.

And if in reply to all this, it be said that the government is expending huge sums in relief, we should remember that it has not taken over the churches, the hospitals, public health nursing, guidance for boys and girls, and a variety of other services which are left to voluntary agencies. Nor can cold impersonal taxation ever be a proper substitute for warm personal sharing of human kindnesses. What may well worry us is that the broadening of governmental relief may make us think we are getting broader in sympathy while in reality we may be growing narrower in our brotherly love.

The fact is we are now in a fighting divisive mood. According to the Institute for Propaganda Analysis, there are now in this country over eight hundred "anti" organizations motivated by the spirit of opposition to some other group or groups. Madison Square Garden could be filled repeatedly by meetings of protest against the Nazis, the Jews, the Japanese or some other current target of hatred. But all the while missionary budgets are shrinking and Chinese relief is receiving a mere fraction of what was given to the Armenians twenty years ago. In short we are organizing around our hatreds rather than around our loves.

In such a situation can we claim to know the breadth of love in any truly Christian sense? Here are a few simple tests: Are we broad enough to be interested in the welfare of those who live on the other side of the railroad tracks? Broad enough to have a heartache when we hear about another disaster in China? Broad enough to resist the race prejudice which is poisoning Europe and threatening to invade America? Broad enough to think of the hungry when we pray, "Give us this day our daily bread"?

Turn now to the second dimension of love—its *length*. To what lengths will we go in showing our brotherhood? In his service to others, the Christian is commanded to go the second mile; in his forgiveness, he is bidden to repeat it "seventy times seven." In true love the sky is the limit. It has no wages-and-hours schedule.

Measured alongside such descriptions, our little loves seem so pathetically lacking in length. In our personal relationships we so often lack the patience and perseverance to carry through our experiments in friendships. In our charities we seldom take the pains to follow through our gifts. Often we give merely to get rid of the request or to keep our own social standing rather than in any real concern to help the recipient to his feet. The roads

THE LIMITS OF LOVE

of life are strewn with the wreckage of run-down and half-finished loves.

We speak of falling in love as if it were something to which we are drawn by the natural gravity of desire. Some love is of that type. But others have to be fought into rather than fallen into. To reach them we must overcome our natural inertia, we must often struggle through our first dislikes. "It is more blessed to give than to receive," but that is not the way it strikes a person when he starts giving. The first stages of giving are frequently painful, but there comes a point in the process where duty is transformed into delight.

To what length will we go, for instance, in our love of country? In time of emergency, to be sure, we may share with Nathan Hale the feeling of regret that we have but one life to give. But such trigger-like bursts of devotion do not last in the prosaic duties of peace. When America was appealing for recruits and liberty-bond buyers in 1917, the countryside was plastered with war posters depicting a woman with a mailed fist at her throat. In the heat of patriotic fervor we personalized our country into a mother and we talked about defending "*her*" honor. But when peace came we depersonalized "mother country" into "the government," we changed the pronoun from "her" to "its," and the adjectives we applied depended on our politics. A few years ago a Wellesley College dean asked whether I thought it would ever be possible to arouse in peace time a patriotic devotion comparable to that which was displayed on her campus during the war. In those stirring days, she said, the students were organized into a unity of spirit wherein they forgot their campus rivalries and petty differences. Yes, we fuse well at fighting temperature, in the heat of fear and anger. But our democracies have not demonstrated much pulling power in peacetime patriotism. Unless we can lead our citizens to lengths of sacrifice for democratic ideals similar to those inspired by totalitarian states, it is not hard to foresee which will forge ahead.

How long must love be to meet the Christian requirements? Here are a few simple concrete tests: To what lengths are we going in forgiving those who will not forgive us? Have we learned to like anyone this past year whom we disliked before? Are we continuing to bet on the best in any persons whom others have given up as hopeless? How far have we gone in trying to save the love in a home which seemed headed for the rocks? How does our willingness to sacrifice for a public project compare with our efforts to gain our private ends?

Consider now the third dimension of love—its *depth*. We may boast a broad spirit of brotherhood and yet be lacking in depth. Much so-called tolerance today is only a shallow indifference in matters about which we do not care deeply. Less concerned about creeds, we are more broadly tolerant toward other religious sects; more sensitive in our purses, we are manifesting a growing intolerance toward other economic and racial groups.

Also, we may go to great lengths in love and yet be so superficial that we do more harm than good. Many an indulgent parent will persevere in providing for his child but not use sufficient intelligence to develop the roots of his character. Or take the case of a devoted but shallow wife pictured by a recent writer. She kept constantly urging her husband to think of himself and his own comfort rather than of the persons and objects for which he was ready to sacrifice himself. "This kind of thing," said the writer, "dropped every day like the lump of sugar into the breakfast cup of tea, in the end produces a constitutional change in the man's mind. He begins to think of himself first as somewhat of a hero when he goes against his wife's sweet counsel, and then a Quixote and then a fool." Thus others have nursed their loved ones into a softening selfishness.

Love in our turbulent and troubled time must be deep enough to get below superficial sentimentalism to realistic sentiment. The shallows of emotion can be churned up into muddy thinking by any gust of popular passion. True friendship has depth enough to keep silent when emotions lie too deep for words. True patriotism sees deeply enough to recognize that the real resources of a country lie not in military equipment quickly outmoded but in the resourcefulness and contentment of its sturdy citizenry, that the national frontiers to be developed are vertical rather than horizontal, that the genuine servants of a country are not the patrioteers prodding the passions with big boasts but the quiet citizens working for peace and public welfare.

The love needed now must have depth enough to root out the causes of evil instead of shooting at the evil-doers. When motion pictures were in their infancy, a little weekly serial appeared under the intriguing title, "The Perils of Pauline." Each week the lovely heroine was brought to the brink of death at the hands of the villain, and then at the crucial moment the film was suspended until the following week. When this little flickering cinema was shown in the western ranch towns, the cowboys, who were not familiar with the workings of motion pictures, often became so excited that they pulled their pistols from their holsters and shot at the villain on the screen. Now, of course, if the irate ranchers had really wished to stop the picture they should have shot into the projector. Their misguided anger was symbolic of many a social attitude. We shoot at the villains projected before the public instead of attacking the causes which produce them. We killed the Huns twenty years ago but we kept the war system. We hate the sinner but keep the sin. The Master never made that mistake. He attacked the roots of the sin while continuing to love the sinner.

Here are a few soundings to test the depth of love: Is it deep enough to withhold from our loved ones the immediate wish if thereby we can insure the larger work? Deep enough to cut with a kindly surgery when nothing else will remove the causes of evil? Deep enough in our charity to wish to hide the gift lest the act of giving may hurt the receiver, in short, to put charitableness into our charity? Deep enough to seek to remove the economic causes of war even though their roots run into our own business and community? Deep enough in our love of God to bear a cross as well as to bow before one?

Let us glance now at the apostle's fourth dimension of love—its *height*. How can we lift ourselves from the present low level of brotherhood to the high plane expected of Christian love? Recall the reason on which Jesus based his injunction of brotherly love. He said, "Love your enemies, bless them that curse you, do good to them that hate you . . . that ye may be the children of your Father which is in heaven; for he maketh his sun to rise on the evil and on the good, and sendeth rain on the just and on the unjust." [2] The Master here uses on a large scale a principle which we can see applied in family relationships. How does an older child learn to care for the newly born infant which comes to share his playthings and his patrimony? By catching from the parents the love which they shower on the little one. Parental affection creates the atmosphere in which love between children flourishes. So in society at large, belief in Divine Fatherhood undergirds and sustains the feeling of human brotherhood.

When we think of what human beings mean to God we cannot think of them as cheap. Every individual is seen not only as some mother's son, precious in her sight, but as a Heavenly Father's child, bought with a price, the high price of sacrificial love symbolized in the cross. When we view men in the light of divine love, then racial distinctions appear as part of a plan for the enrichment of mankind, each race bringing its unique contribution to the world's culture. Coöperation between races then moves not like a stream flowing down condescendingly from higher to lower, but as the tide moves across the bosom of the deep, that is, on the level drawn by the attraction of a heavenly power above.

[2] Matthew 5: 44, 45.

Only in an atmosphere charged with spiritual understanding and passion could be struck these lines by Florence Kiper Frank, entitled:

### The Jew to Jesus [3]

O man of my own people, I alone
Among these alien ones can know thy face,
I who have felt the kinship of our race
Burn in me as I sit where they intone
Thy praises—those who, striving to make known
A god for sacrifice, have missed the grace
Of thy sweet human meaning in its place,
Thou who art of our blood-bond and our own.

Are we not sharers of thy Passion! Yea,
In spirit-anguish closely by thy side
We have drained the bitter cup and, tortured, felt
With thee the bruising of each heavy welt.
In every land is our Gethsemane.
A thousand times have we been crucified.

In his best seller of some years ago, "If Winter Comes," A. S. M. Hutchinson created a character, Mark Sabre, who took this high ground of brotherhood. An unfortunate betrayed girl was cast upon the mercy of his household. She was no relative. She had no claim upon him, except that she was a fellow human being in need. To aid her would involve personal sacrifice and risk to his reputation. Yet Mark Sabre reasoned with himself thus: "Here was a human creature come to us . . . breathing the same air, sharing the same mortality, responsible to the same God. If you've got a grain, a jot of

[3] Printed by kind permission of the author.

humanity you must out of the very flesh and bone of you respond to the cry of one made as you yourself are made." Pretty high ground to take? Yes, but it is the level of Christ-like love, and nothing lower will get us above the conflicts which rage around our lesser loyalties.

# Chapter IX

# LOCKING OURSELVES OUT

WHICH is worse, to be shut in or to be shut out? If a Gallup poll were taken in America, it would probably reveal a greater dread of the former than of the latter, for if there is any one thing which we Americans seem to want above others, it is freedom. The young crave the chance to live their own lives. Women are still fighting to free themselves from the handicaps put on their sex by our man-made social order. Men rebel against the regimentation of their work and business. And we prize our liberties the more highly because of the loss of freedom now being suffered on foreign shores.

Nevertheless, we repeat the question: Which is worse, to be locked in or to be locked out? Consider the home where a daughter feels herself restricted by the rigid rules of her parents. Dreadfully disagreeable, yes. But is it as bad as being an orphan without a home to which one can turn for sympathy and guidance? Or think of the husband who is tied to a nagging wife. Bad, yes. But, after all, is his situation quite so pathetic as that of an Enoch Arden, who returns to look from the outside at a home from which he is shut out? Or take the American citizen who feels the irritations of his tax burden and resents the legal fences limiting his free enterprise. Unpleasant, perhaps unwholesome, but is is half so bad as to be one of the German refugees, men without a country?

Firmly embedded in our thinking is the fear of losing

our liberties, but no less clearly should we consider the danger of locking ourselves out—a danger which threatens us through certain tendencies now apparent.

For one thing, we may lock ourselves out of tomorrow's full life by *standing in our own way*.

In October, 1842, Emerson entered in his Journal this sentence: "Henry Thoreau made last night the fine remark that as long as a man stands in his own way, everything seems to be in his way." One of the most common blunders is to blame others for blocking our paths, when in reality we are standing in our own way. The spoiled child comes to think that every rule of the household is a hampering restriction on his own happiness. The more rope he is given, the more he complains that it is choking him. The housekeeper who dwells only on her own desires finds her duties seemingly more burdensome, no matter how many labor-saving devices may be at her disposal; and because so many wives and husbands make such a point of standing on their rights, light housekeeping and comfortable homes do not save families from the divorce court. The libertine who puts his own desires and appetites first soon comes to look upon all social decencies and moral codes as old-fashioned, narrow-minded Puritanical blue laws. Breaking the rules of his own self-control, he blames all the laws of social control. The lawless individualist whose idea of personal liberty is license to do as he pleases considers every form of government a barrier to his freedom. Constitutions may be amended or repealed, institutions of government may be liberalized or socialized, but still the anarchistic egoist is not satisfied.

Yes, when we are standing in our own way, we always think someone else is stopping us. And in this fact is to be found one of the root causes for personal unhappiness and social unrest. As individuals and groups and nations we talk interminably about standing on our rights, and in that attitude we seldom see our opportunities and almost never see our duties.

Granted that there are too many laws cluttering our statute books, that there are piratical forces hindering us in our business pursuits, that there are bandit nations blocking the roads to world peace, can we honestly say that if all these obstacles were removed the way would then be clear for our inalienable rights of "life, liberty, and the pursuit of happiness"? No, there would still remain our own restless, stubborn, short-sighted selves standing in the way. Suppose that we could remove the economic barriers which shut off so many of our citizens from the abundant life, and guarantee financial security to every person within our national domain, there would still remain those inner personal problems around which Shakespeare and Eugene O'Neill have woven their plots. Admitting that social environment and physical heredity play an almost immeasurable part in shaping our way of living, nevertheless when a person offers those external factors as the complete alibi for his misconduct, there is in him not much hope of reform.

In view of all this, the Master's way to the good life is to get out of our own way before beginning to nudge the fellow next to us. Jesus lived under a dictator, yet he did not start his redemptive work by launching a political revolution to dethrone Caesar and his Roman deputies who held Palestine in throttle. He lived in a land which was overrun by foreigners, yet he did not blame his country's ills on them. No, Jesus even used a foreigner, a Samaritan, to drive home a principle of brotherliness which would stir his own countrymen to contrition. The Master's method of moving toward the free life is to start by getting out of our own way first.

A second way whereby we lock ourselves out of tomorrow's larger life is by *stressing what belongs to us rather than what we belong to.*

"A man's life consisteth not in the abundance of things which he possesseth." [1] Rather, it consists far more in the abundance and quality of the things to which he belongs. Do we Americans need any encouragement in this matter of belonging? We have been laughed at as a nation of joiners. Mr. Mencken thought he found in this trait a most vulnerable spot for his rapier of ridicule. And when one thinks of the lodges and clubs which clutter our social circles and the costumes and paraphernalia which parade through convention cities, he is inclined to a revulsion against joiners. But these multiplied organizations are a manifestation of our *desire* for belongings rather than for actually belonging. Membership in them is seldom motivated by a deep devotion which turns the current of life from getting to giving. We add badges to our lapels, but we do not give our hearts to great commitments.

One of the paradoxical laws of living is that a person does not get the true wealth which belongs to him until he feels a deep sense of belonging. Take it in the home.

[1] Luke 12: 15.

We have very properly come to recognize the rights of the individual in the family. We have reacted from the old tendency to treat the child as the property of the parent. The ideal of the modern home is a partnership of free minds in which the experiences of the elders supplement and guide the experiments of the younger. But when the individual rather than the family is made the unit, the process may be carried so far that the child never learns how to gear himself into the group action of the home nor to subordinate his will to the welfare of the family. In so far as this happens, the child is being deprived of something which belongs to him as his birthright in the family, for our family birthright consists not primarily in a share of the estate, but in a sharing of the disciplines and responsibilities which make the home. The lad who misses this experience of belonging suffers a loss far greater than a financial one.

Similarly in marriage many lock themselves out of its satisfactions by looking too intently at their rights—a tendency accentuated by the economic independence of women and the pressure which pushes both husband and wife into the business of bread-earning. When two persons treat their home as a sort of convenience to serve the interests of each, when the husband considers the home mainly as a comfortable place to step into from the stress of business, and when the wife thinks of the home as a convenient place to step out from with a security not shared by her unmarried women friends—when such is the spirit of the marriage contract, it is not long before both begin to feel cheated in their bargain. When a member of the family falls into the mood of wondering whether he is getting out of it all that belongs to him, he is pretty sure to feel imposed on; but when he devotes himself to giving the family what belongs to it, he enjoys a growing sense of gratitude for the privilege.

Or turn from the family to the state. Two basic theories of government are in conflict today. On the one side are the fascist states wherein the individual exists for the state. On the other are the democracies in which, theoretically at least, government is of the people and for the people with guarantee of civil and religious liberty to every citizen. True it is that Jesus treated individuals as ends in themselves, never as means to an end, and governments, like the Sabbath, are made for man and not man for governments. Democracy and Christianity stand together on the basic principle of safeguarding the values of individual personality.

Nevertheless in our insistence on individual rights are we in danger of stressing what the government is to do for us and forgetting what we are to do for the state? When some months ago I watched the boys in Berlin marching in hosts through the streets, I was saddened by the thought that they were prospective cannon fodder commandeered for destruction by dictatorial governments. But I am also saddened when I see how many groups in America march on Washington to get the government to do something for them. It is damnable when citizens are used by their totalitarian governments as cannon fodder. It is also damnable when democratic governments are used by their citizens as pork barrels.

Furthermore I have to confess that there was a gleam in the eyes of those marching boys in Berlin which I have not always caught on the sidewalks of New York. The dictators with all their evils have succeeded in kindling a glow of fervor which the democracies have not yet duplicated.

In the state, as in the family, the paradoxical truth is that we do not get what belongs to us until we have a sense of belonging. At present we are tending to lock ourselves out of these blessings by personal, sectional selfish interests. And if our free countries are not to be outstripped by the blustering fascist nations across the sea, we need a rebirth of patriotism; not of the subservient, dictated type; not of the narrow, nationalistic kind; not of the swashbuckling, sword-swinging variety, but a patriotism as zealous for peace as men have been for war, a patriotism that can enlist youth in constructive causes as the lads of Germany are aroused by their imperialistic dreams. What are democracy's substitutes for the rallying cries of the dictators? What big things are we free peoples living for? What causes stir us to a unifying zeal? It takes big objectives to call forth the greatness of a people. We in America must rethink our desires for freedom until we discover that the largest liberty comes from belonging rather than from belongings.

When we turn from the secular to the spiritual realm, we find that we are locking ourselves out of the largest religious values because we lack this sense of belonging. Too many of us in America think of the church not as a great spiritual mother to which we belong, but rather as a sort of local institution set up to serve community needs. This attitude is due in part to our national inheritance. The pioneers brought their denominations with them to their new settlements. The churches having been moved in, do not give the impression of being rooted in time immemorial, as do the ancient shrines of Europe. When the traveler approaches an Old World town, he beholds the secular buildings clustered about, and dominated by the cathedral, as chickens gather about a mother hen. In our American cities the church buildings are overshadowed by the secular structures and are moved about to keep up with changing residential sections. Thus the youth and mobility of our churches accentuate the popular feeling of the church as a social institution rather than a spiritual mother.

And in a very legitimate sense God and his church are for men's use. "The Son of man came not to be ministered unto, but to minister." [2] The church erected in his name is an agency for serving human needs. We go to it for the servicing of our spirits when our batteries of courage and faith are run down. We go to the church for fellowship in loneliness and for aid in adversity. We call upon it to train our children in those virtues which make for the good life.

Nevertheless it is also true that these services are never fully appropriated by those who merely try to use them, but only by those who are willing to be used for God's purposes. The spiritual paradox is that God can give his power only to those who are giving their power to him. This transfer of power proceeds by a principle apparent elsewhere, in music for instance. A piano or violin is an instrument to be used, and a musician may use such instruments to give himself pleasure or to earn income.

[2] Matthew 20: 28.

But the greatest satisfaction and thrill are gotten when the player forgets himself in surrender to the theme he is interpreting. Similarly in religious experience, it is by being used rather than by trying to use that we get the deepest satisfactions.

The persons who go into a group for what they can get out of it usually get out of it rather quickly because they do not receive as much as they expected. To coin an expression, these may be called the "get-outers." And they usually begin as the "go-getters."

This brash utilitarian attitude toward the church must be corrected by a mellowing sense of its age and authority. When we essay to measure its service we must evaluate it as we would a mighty river. We would not measure the value of the Mississippi merely by counting the tonnage it carries or the electric power generated along its course. We would think also of the swamps it has drained, the fields it has made fertile, the hearts its scenery has gladdened through the ages. So with the church, its service is not to be measured by the statistics of its organizations, but it must be thought of as an ageless, mighty stream of godliness flowing down from the mountains of religious experience, draining the swamps of sin, making the fruits of the spirit to grow. Viewed in that light, the church is seen not as tributary to our secular interests, but as the stream along which our towns and towers have grown up.

In the decade ahead no more decisive question confronts us than the relation between church and state. Is the church to be used again as a mere adjunct of the state as it was twenty years ago—used to sanctify imperial aims, its pulpits as recruiting stations, its sacred symbols held before the eyes of dying boys, killed to defend national "honor"? How long can religious institutions so subservient command the respect of the people? Unless we make God sovereign, we cannot make him saving. Governments as well as individuals must heed the truth delivered by Dostoyevsky, "*A man who bows down to nothing can never bear the burden of himself.*"

*Chapter X*

## AMERICA'S NEW HORIZONS

WHEN the late Justice Oliver Wendell Holmes reached his ninetieth birthday, rich in honors, still in possession of his powers, he received many tributes. Of him Chief Justice Hughes said that he had attained "the most beautiful and rarest thing in the world . . . a complete life." Yet with all the apparent completeness of such a well-rounded life, Justice Holmes, in a letter of thanks to the Federal Bar Association, wrote: "Life seems to me like a Japanese picture which our imagination does not allow to end with the margin. We aim at the Infinite and when our arrow falls to earth, it is in flames."

All great living is inspired by the lift of a vista beyond the attained, yes, beyond the attainable. When the writer of the Epistle to the Hebrews lists the noble men of faith who hang in Israel's Hall of Fame, he portrays them thus: "These all died in faith, not having received the promises, but having seen them afar off, and were persuaded of them, and embraced them, and confessed that they were strangers and pilgrims on the earth." [1] Thus he has left those ancient worthies limned against the horizon of history like mountain climbers, peering ever toward promises higher than their reach, dying in faith, still on the upward trend.

We are the spiritual heirs of those Old Testament heroes of faith, and of the New World's intrepid pioneers.

[1] Hebrews 11: 13.

We shall be unworthy of our tradition and wasters of our inheritance unless we move out of the mood of indecision which now halts us. Our present lack of confidence may very probably be due, as Walter Lippmann points out, to the failure of the three great experiments tried during the last twenty years, viz., the efforts to establish an enduring peace, to restore the world's economy, and to secure an abundant life through a "New Deal" at home.[2] Having tried three times and failed, disillusioned America is now inclined to withdraw into isolation, bury her gold, curtail her crops, and suspend her reforms. But the American eagle cannot become an ostrich. God has given us the richest resources and the turn of world events has whirled us into the place of potential leadership. Unless we arouse ourselves to attempt the great things which ought to be done, we shall not be able to do the smaller things which we wish to do. By striving toward the impossible perfections, we are helped to perfect the possible.

Louis Bromfield gave the background of his book "Possession" in the words of one of his characters, a young man: "My grandfathers came into this wilderness to conquer and subdue it. It was a land filled with savages and adventure. I too must have my chance. I am of a race of pioneers but I no longer have any frontier." In those words the youth was giving voice to the yeasty feeling of restlessness which was stirring in the early post-war period. Now youth, as well as the rest of us, seems to be looking for security rather than frontiers. But we must and we shall recover the exploring pioneering spirit. Our

[2] *Life,* June 5, 1939.

frontiers are no longer geographical. They are social, spiritual, vertical.

How will the American spiritual tradition face these new social horizons? We are now old enough as a nation to have developed some distinctive traditions. We have our own folklore, our antiques, our architecture. And although our religious heritage roots in the Old World, the transplanted shoots have taken on characteristics peculiarly American.

In appraising the spirituality of early America we must be realistic. The settlers were not all saints, even though some bore the name of Puritans. The religious motives of the American colonists were of course mixed with commercial interests. But by and large there was a pervasive sense of God's sovereignty. They looked upon their new homes as veritably God-given.

Out of a lawyer's office some time ago came a rather luminous bit of humor. A New York law firm was trying to clear the title of some New Orleans property and asked a New Orleans attorney to undertake the job. The New Orleans attorney traced it back to 1803, but the New York lawyer countered with a reply to the effect that this was not quite far enough back. An answering letter came from New Orleans in this fashion: "Please be advised that in the year 1803 the United States of America acquired the Territory of Louisiana from the Republic of France by purchase; the Republic of France had, in turn, acquired title from the Spanish Crown by conquest; the Spanish Crown having originally acquired title by virtue of the discoveries of one Christopher Columbus, a Genoese sailor, who had been duly authorized to embark upon his voyages of discovery by Isabella, Queen of Spain; Isabella, before granting such authority, had obtained the sanction of His Holiness, the Pope; the Pope is the Vicar on earth of Jesus Christ; Jesus Christ is the Son and Heir Apparent of God; God made Louisiana!" Beneath the humor of that document lies the truth that the settlers recognized a divine ownership antedating the royal arms emblazoned on their settlements.

And on this new continent our forefathers evolved what we call "the American way of life," an expression recently come to emphasis. It is a way of life wherein every person at birth is endowed with the "inalienable rights of life, liberty and the pursuit of happiness," which rights he is to exercise subject only to those social regulations necessary to insure the same privileges to others. The American way of life is one wherein all men are equal before God and the government, not equal in ability but each one good enough to have a say in choosing the best. It is a way wherein the majority rules yet accords every minority the right to promote its views by the peaceful arts of persuasion. It is a way wherein each person enjoys the right to worship God according to the dictates of his own conscience, wherein parents are still free to educate their children without the regimentation of any autocratic government, and youth is still able to plan its own careers without the intervention of any dictator.

"The essence of the American system is that it has no dogmatic purpose, that it is not a system at all, but a way of life in which men proceed by unending inquiry and debate, having agreed to agree as best they can, because there is no other way they can combine freedom with order." [3]

And now the American way faces a world vitally different from that of its founders. How will the salient traits of our national tradition fare in the world of tomorrow?

Consider the emphasis on national independence, a note stressed more than ever in these days of the Old World's entanglements. It seemed feasible in the time of Benjamin Franklin to talk about escaping England's burdensome taxes, by retiring into a self-subsisting life on the vast American continent. But we cannot step out of the world of radio and airplane into isolation. However much we might wish that our neighbors would mind their own business and leave us to mind ours, we are caught in the currents of world interdependence. What affects the industries of Japan and Australia affects the markets of Kansas City and Chicago. As our Secretary of State has said, "If goods cannot cross boundaries, troops soon will." And the currents of thought are even more impossible to escape. The air waves carry their messages across national boundaries. Ideas, art, culture are no respecters of nations.

Since the world's life washes our shores, we cannot wash our hands of world responsibilities. Some years ago, in the city of Athens, I met an American who had been a relief worker among the Armenians during the Turkish atrocities. He had been beaten on the soles of his feet until he could not walk for six months, one of his

[3] "The Obligation of the Universities to the Social Order." New York University Press, 1933, p. 456.

co-workers had been driven stark mad and another killed. I said to him, "Aren't you bitter toward the Turks?" "No," he answered, "not particularly, for I cannot see how in the eyes of Christian morality it is much worse to kill a man than it is to let a man be killed when you could save him. The Turks killed, but the Christian nations stood by and let them do it." Rather a nice question, isn't it? How much worse is it to kill a man than to let a man be killed when you could save him?

America, the most powerful nation in the world, cannot play Pilate when lives and ideals are being slaughtered. To say this, however, does not mean that we should throw our resources or troops into the present mess of power politics seething in Europe. If America can keep as neutral as possible, she will be in better position to lead in the coöperative peace program of tomorrow. For we must remember that there is a difference between destructive alliances for war and constructive coöperation for peace. The United States can and should take the lead in encouraging trade with the sane, peace-loving nations, in working for open markets, in summoning a world economic conference, and in opening cultural avenues of good will. The two most powerful voices for peace in the world today are those of the Pope at Rome and the President at Washington, even though at the moment they have failed to halt Hitler.

But leadership in the coöperative peace program of tomorrow requires clean hands. In a most remarkable broadcast to the country on May 8, 1935, Admiral William S. Sims said: "The point of the whole business is this, we cannot keep out of a war and at the same time enforce the freedom of the seas—that is, the freedom to make profits out of countries engaged in a death struggle. If a war arises, we must therefore choose between two courses: between great profits, with grave risks of war, on the one hand; or smaller profits and less risk, on the other. When I say 'we' I mean not only the traders themselves but all of us, for practically our whole population benefited by this wartime trade—though we did not understand that we were inviting disaster for ourselves and for the world. . . . We, as a people, must come to understand that peace is priceless; that it is worth any reasonable sacrifice of war profits; that a decent regard for humanity must be placed ahead of gold. Therefore, let every citizen who has the cause of honorable peace at heart take this stand: Our trade as a neutral must be at the risk of the traders; our army and navy must not be used to protect this trade. It is a choice of profits or peace. Our country must remain at peace." [4]

America can best serve the cause of peace right now by demonstrating the successful working of the democratic system, free from industrial exploitation at home and from imperial exploitation abroad. To send force to the defense of the democratic ideal would be not only futile in its effect *beyond* our borders, but also fatal to democracy *within* our borders. The only way to make democracy really safe is to make it work, and the only way to make it work is to keep it out of war.

Consider now a second trait evolved and emphasized by the American tradition, that of our personal inde-

---

[4] Quoted by Charles A. Beard and Mary R. Beard in "America in Midpassage." Macmillan, 1939, p. 429.

pendence. Liberty is the life-blood of the American way.
We encourage it in our homes. We develop it in our
schools. We are trending toward further freedom in our
churches. The agencies of public opinion have to pay at
least lip service to the liberty-loving public.

Yet freedom is not a simple single concept. There is
national liberty, which is freedom from foreign domina-
tion; and there is political liberty, which is freedom from
despotic government. Both of these we enjoy in America. But what about economic liberty, that is, freedom
of the ordinary man from the limitations imposed by
poverty and bad environment? How free are the "Okies"
driven from the frying pan of the dust bowl into the fire
of Imperial Valley, where abject hunger forces them to
take whatever paltry wage the corporate farmers and
their hosts of improvised deputy sheriffs deign to pay?
Writing a separate opinion in the case of the New York
minimum wage law for women, Justice Stone, on June 1,
1936, said: "There is grim irony in speaking of the freedom of contract of those who, because of their economic
necessities, give their services for less than is needful to
keep body and soul together."

And what about a fourth form of liberty, the personal
freedom of the individual to think, speak and act as he
will? We pride ourselves on our freedom of thought, but
observation would lead to the belief that the man on the
street is about as free in his thinking as the stray dog who
follows any chance passer-by. Vagrant thinking is really
not independent thought. Furthermore, true freedom of
thought requires also freedom of knowledge, a thing
which is denied in regimented countries. Dictators are

willing to allow their subjects the utmost liberty of thinking as long as they control the supply of facts. Hitler encourages literacy with the same energy which Thomas Jefferson showed, but for a different purpose. The autocrats desire a citizenry able to read so that they can devour the propaganda which is fed to them. Ostensibly, in America, we have freedom of knowledge as well as freedom of thought, but in our deluge of propaganda the plain man finds difficulty in discerning the truth, and most will not make the effort.

Freedom of speech faces the new frontiers of the air. It was one thing for the stump speaker to be at liberty to say what he thought when he was heard only by those who came to hear him. It is somewhat different when one's voice is dropped without warning into the heart of a home or across a national boundary. The air channels must be kept free, but their users must interpret that liberty with a heightened intelligence and imagination.

Freedom of conscience was safeguarded by our founding fathers primarily through fear that some religious group might gain dominance over the state. Now the danger to be feared is not dominance by some church but regimentation by the state. With the fingers of government spreading to every phase of life, we must be on our guard lest they reach in to throttle the preacher, and especially the teacher. It is fundamental that teachers shall be free in their religious, social and political affiliations and secure in their tenure from group pressures.

Freedom of action is not the same thing on the motorized highway as in the horse and buggy era. We cannot loiter through the Holland Tunnel or chat with the neighbors we meet in four-lane traffic. Liberty must become acclimated to the crowd if it is to survive.

Or take a third characteristic of the American way, individual enterprise. The frontier encouraged personal resourcefulness. In fact, it made such self-reliance necessary to survival. The land lay open to invite individual initiative and the sky was the limit of its reward. When our colonies were forming themselves into a nation, the prevailing political philosophy was that of Voltaire, Rousseau, Tom Paine and their school, namely, that man was able to master his own destiny, with little help from government or from God.

But our traditional rugged individualism is now up against something still more rugged, a machine age, and under its pressure we are being driven to discard the old economic Darwinism. It is to be hoped that we have at last repudiated the idea that poverty and unemployment are due to the improvident and evil lives of the poor. Twelve million Americans can't be wrong. Our Puritan virtues of thrift, sobriety and industry, which do make for personal success, led us into the fallacy of making prosperity and piety too nearly synonymous. It now behooves us to christianize the power we have achieved and to relieve the poverty we have produced.

With all our individualism, we are ready enough to call in the government to deliver us from our distresses, but we are loath to let it interfere with our successes. One of our subtlest and most baffling problems is how to create organizations necessary for effective social action, and yet to preserve the individual initiative essential to vital personal living. Our present penchant for organizing carries us rather far. As one of our publicists recently said, "If three Americans fell out of an airplane, they would be organized before they reached the ground into a president, a secretary, and a treasurer." And then we fall into the error of thinking that the organization will do the trick we want done. Thus, group action endangers individual initiative and responsibility. We cannot deny that public relief does sometimes cut the nerve of personal enterprise. We are also aware of the increasing tendency to let the government do what individuals ought to do for themselves. We know that as cities and churches grow in size, personal participation often shrinks, with the result that our large cities have usually worse political systems than our smaller towns, and our large churches lack the per capita enthusiasm of the small pioneer parishes.

This dwarfing pressure of numbers and organization not only cuts the nerve of democracy; it also kills the zest of personal living. We do not feel the thrill of any enterprise unless we give play to the personal explorative, creative element. How to keep the creative feeling of the old pioneer worker in the factory conditions of to-day? Will it have to be done only in our avocations? How to preserve the zeal of the town meeting in the metropolitan politics of New York or Boston? As Sir Arthur Salter says, we need a "good citizen" policy to supplement a "good neighbor" policy. Being a good neighbor is simpler than being a good citizen. The former means not hurting anyone else, being kind and helpful;

the latter means assuming duties and responsibilities, playing a public part.

But, is being a good neighbor a simple matter? What can preserve the old pioneer spirit of neighborliness in the midst of our modern city life? We cannot leave charity to the personal moods of individual good Samaritans. We must organize our charity and relief and security programs, and yet not lose the personal touch. That is anything but simple.

We can institute organizations and restrictions to curb individualism, but how can we instill personal initiative to curb overweening organization? That is the issue America must face. It means training our citizens to work together in group action for the doing of things we cannot do each for himself. It means training ourselves to do things which organizations cannot and should not do for us. It means "bearing one another's burdens" without lessening the willingness of each to bear his own burdens. Nothing less than a religious motive can safeguard both objectives. Dwight L. Moody was wont to say that character is what a man is in the dark. The statement might well be paraphrased, "character is what a man is in the crowd." And if a person is to stand up to his responsibilities when lost in the crowd, he must be sustained by a divinely inspired sense of duty and a divinely sensitive regard for his neighbor.

Lord Stamp in his radio address to the recent Congress on Education and Democracy raised very earnestly the question of how we are to educate for this social purpose and moral intensity. He said: "Certainly the guarded, professional, artistic, philosophic ethics which form the content of moral behavior and the tepid, respectable, well-bridled enthusiasms which are its impetus, in the intellectual classes from which educators are drawn, are not calculated to fire the imagination, to raise to striking heat, to clarify the imperatives for the mass of mankind. It seems that nothing less than the sacrifice, devotion, dogmatism and supreme personality of a great religion can do that." [5]

A few summers ago I sat one Sunday morning at Mackinac Island in the little park dominated by the statue of Marquette, the missionary and explorer. As I looked at the majestic figure of the man, heroic in its proportions, I began to feel a sense of power radiating from him. Then my eye glanced across the park to a little church with its doors open for the morning service. The summer tourists seemed so heedless of its presence, that after a time I began to feel a sense of pity for the struggling congregation. Then I said to myself: "Here am I, a minister of the Church of Christ. Do I represent something which impresses people with a sense of pity as did that ignored church or with a sense of power as did Marquette?" To many the church is an object of pity, a leader of a lost cause. But the longer I work in the church, although I grow increasingly aware of its weaknesses, the more firmly I feel that it possesses the power which can transform our wilderness of human relations as the pioneers cleared the wilderness of the west.

As the settlers trekked out into the territory of Kansas in order to keep it free from slaves, they sang a hymn which Whittier wrote for them:

[5] Reported in *New York Times*, August 16, 1939.

We cross the prairies as of old
The pilgrims crossed the sea,
To make the West as they the East
The Homestead of the Free.

We go to plant her common schools
On distant prairie swells,
And give the Sabbath of the mind
The music of her bells.

Upbearing like the ark of old
The Bible in our van,
We go to test the truth of God
Against the fraud of man.

We might well keep the mood of that hymn as we
move toward America's new horizons.

# Chapter XI

# THE LAST FRONTIER

Not far from the place in which these lines are written is a church bulletin board bearing a very arresting sentence: "Prepare to meet your God." That striking sentence stirs in me a boyhood memory of a sermon on those words delivered by a woman evangelist in the community where I was reared. The flaming illustrations of that fiery sermon have kept their color across the years. Incident after incident did she relate of persons snatched suddenly from the warm scenes of life to stand before the cold seat of the Last Judgment. No doubt that message arrested many others besides myself with the thought of preparedness for the life hereafter.

Valid and valuable as such sermons may be, I have never felt that the Master would wish his ministers to preach too many of them. Jesus did not issue repeated warnings about death and divine judgment. He proceeded on the principle that if men are ready to meet the crises of life, they will be ready to face the crisis of death. He tried to give men such a confidence in God's world seen and unseen that dying would seem no long leap in the dark.

When I think of the Christlike attitude toward death, I think of a certain feature in a college fraternity initiation. The initiates were led blindfolded to the edge of the sidewalk curb. One of those conducting the initiation told the blindfolded youth that he was standing on the edge of a high precipice and that he would have to show his courage by jumping off into the valley below. It was a frightening moment for the poor fellow whose eyes were bound, but when he jumped or was pushed off, he found that he landed on the street only about eight inches below the level of the curbstone. So death seems a leap in the dark; but Jesus, the comforting guide, unlike the college initiators, fortified his followers by telling them that if they walked his way on this earth, then dying would be merely a stepping from the sidewalk of time into the street of eternal life.

He who learns the good life faces the last frontier unafraid. Does someone say that the truly good life should face death with indifference, unconcerned about its rewards or punishments? One of my former college teachers was accustomed to say rather proudly that he would do his duty and live the same kind of life regardless of what comes after death. But when we hear persons say that death does not count, we feel disposed to ask, "Whose death?" If one is thinking merely of himself, there may be something noble in saying that death is a matter of indifference. But when he stands beside the grave of a loved one, is it noble to say he has no interest in what becomes of the departed? It is love even more than selfishness which cries for eternal life.

Yes, the very sense of life's whole integrity is involved in this matter of immortality. Are we living for a short tomorrow, making our plans as children draw designs on a frosted windowpane, only to have them vanish with the noonday warmth; or are we to be "steadfast, unmovable, always abounding in the work of the Lord, forasmuch as (we) know that (our) labor is not in vain in the Lord"? [1]

May I, therefore, speaking in the first person, share with you some of my reasons for the faith that is in me regarding life's last frontier?

I believe in a life beyond the grave because I believe in the integrity of the human personality.

By a mere physical test, man would be but a bundle of material elements which could be bought today in the store for about a dollar. If we watched him we would see that he moved like other locomotive beings which we call animals. We would see that he is somewhat larger than the ape which he resembles in features, much less clear of eye and dull of ear than some of the beasts of the field, far less strong than the ox, somewhat longer lived than the horse—in short, a moderate-sized, mediocrely equipped animal. Such is a man by the test of the physical senses.

But watch him a bit further. Yonder he goes up the street. What motivates him? Is he hungry and hunting for food? No, he may have just had his lunch. Is he following some object which he sees? No, perhaps he is not observing anything in his environment. Does he scent something in the air which he seeks? No, probably he is not conscious for the moment of any smells. Does he hear something that frightens him from where he was or lures him to where he is going? No, even here in New York a man may walk along the street unmindful of the noise. The incentives which motivate that man may reside not at all in his five physical senses. They may be love, or

[1] I Corinthians 15: 58.

ambition, or hate or their like—invisible all of them, but nevertheless real.

Observe the man further. He reaches a house which he calls home. Its walls are hung with pictures. It is not enough for him to have a den or nest, as the animals do, simply to shelter his body. He has something in him that craves beauty and he will often go without food to buy paintings. Yet paintings are only canvases with colored liquids brushed on them, materials which could be bought for a paltry sum. But an artist with what we call genius put an idea into those paints. Genius, ideas—what are these? Things we cannot handle and see—but nevertheless real, so real that we pay thousands of dollars for them.

It is Christmas Eve and our man joins with a group of little children who call him father, and around a blazing hearth they sing "Holy Night." Strange sounds those would seem to an animal. Trifling sensations they would be when measured by material tests—merely wave pulsations in the air beating against the ear drum. But can you thus appraise the emotions and meaning of that song as sung by little children in the ears of their father? No, something is let loose into the atmosphere which we cannot reach with the senses but which is nevertheless real, so real that some of us would give about all we possess to experience it again.

The most valuable and powerful elements in man's life here are invisible and intangible. Strange being this which we call man—which keeps pursuing unseen urges, peering around the corners of tomorrow to discover whither he is going. Weird power is this which the imagination possesses enabling a man to build his castles in Spain while he is laying bricks in the Bronx. Someone has put into man "such stuff as dreams are made of." Someone has made him but "little lower than the angels." Dust are these bodies, and to dust they return, but in this earthy house of our habitation there is something that

> Leaps life's narrow bars
> To claim its birthright with the hosts of heaven!

A novelist of our day chides the Christian faith by saying that while man calls himself a child of God, he lives like an ape digging for ground nuts. Alas, we do sometimes live like animals. But there are times when we do not. Have you ever been in a zoo when a fire broke out? The bedlam of terror in the monkey cage is bloodcurdling. But a few years ago the airship *Akron* took fire during a fierce electrical storm over the Atlantic seaboard. In that great dirigible were men caught like animals in a cage. The lightning flashes, like the torches of hell, illumined the frightful night and the falling ship, but the ruins revealed that the men had stood at their posts of duty. Do apes stand heroically at their posts of duty when fire comes devouringly toward them? Do apes rush into burning buildings to save the offspring of other beasts? Do apes lay down their lives for their friends, to say nothing of their enemies? When we see what men die *of*, we recognize that our bodies have an animal structure; but when we see what men die *for*, we realize that life is more than meat.

Whence came those ideals for which men are willing to die? Was it from the dust that Socrates derived his sense of duty which caused him to drink the hemlock rather than run away? Was it from the earth that Jesus of Nazareth drew the love which led him to the cross and made him say, "Father, forgive them" as they drove the nails through his hands? Certainly duty, love, hope and their like come not out of the material elements which make up our bodies.

Man is more than the sum of his senses. "Feeling, purposes, values make up our consciousness as much as sense-impressions. We follow up the sense-impressions and find that they lead into an external world discussed by science; we follow up the other elements of our being and find that they lead—not into a world of space and time, but surely somewhere." So speaks one of the most quoted scientists of our day, Professor A. S. Eddington of Cambridge. And because I believe with him that these invisible elements are an integral part of life here and must lead somewhere, I am disposed to believe in the possibility of a life beyond the realm of time and space.

A second ground for my belief in the life hereafter is that I believe in the integrity of this universe, even where I cannot see. There are times, I confess, in which I am inclined to doubt the honesty of this world order. I have had friends struck down by accidents through no fault of their own. I have seen towns destroyed by hurricanes and homes shaken down by earthquakes. I have seen the wicked prosper and the good suffer, and I too have felt that life is "a tale told by an idiot, full of sound and fury, signifying nothing."

But I have always been put to shame in such moods by two groups of persons, the great sufferers who through all their pain have preserved a belief in a beneficent Providence, and the great scientists who, while not talking about spiritual matters, have demonstrated an amazing confidence in the dependability of this physical universe.

An American astronomer some few years ago observed certain movements in the heavenly bodies which could not be accounted for by anything which had yet been discovered. But knowing that the laws of the heavens are dependable, he reasoned from what he could see to what he could not see, and announced to the world his belief that there was another planet swimming yonder somewhere in those illimitable spaces. Years passed. The scientist died. But the time came when one of our powerful telescopes picked up conclusive evidence of that shy heavenly stranger.

Science, the queen to whose sway our modern world now stands so subject, does not hesitate to declare her belief in things she has not seen on the basis of things she has seen. In fact, it is thus and only thus that science has enlarged her domain. Suppose that scientists had never seen a body of water, did not know that there were oceans, or lakes, or rivers, and an eagle should drop into their midst a fish. Those men of science, studying the gill-breathing apparatus of the fish, would conclude that here was an animal designed to live in some other environment than dry land, and they would thereupon agree that there must be somewhere such a medium.

Just as science postulates a gas to explain the phenomena of the laboratory, or a new planet to explain the

movements of the stars, or a body of water to explain
the existence of fish, why is it not the part of wisdom
to believe that there must be a land which "eye hath not
seen and ear hath not heard," in order to explain the
presence in man of the persistent and universal inclina-
tion towards it? For "this longing after immortality" is
a normal appetite of the human soul, felt by the best
minds in their healthiest moments. It is universal, being
found among all races. It is persistent, haunting the
twentieth century sage as well as the primitive savage.
Can it be that the universe which keeps faith with the
instincts of the bird by providing air in which to fly and
with the instincts of the fish by furnishing water in
which to swim has played most cruelly false to man by
endowing him with this craving for eternity only to
deny its gratification? A heavenless universe would seem
to be as deceptive and dishonest as a foodless one. And
if this is a non-moral world order, how can we explain
the rise of moral aspiration in man? It needs a moral
universe and immortal life to explain man. The integrity
of the universe would seem to be at stake in this matter
of immortality.

A third reason for my belief in the life hereafter is that
I believe in the integrity of Jesus of Nazareth.

As one of the six hundred million who look to Jesus
as the Lord of life, I am impressed with his absolute sin-
cerity and honesty as a teacher. When I see the young
carpenter come back from his baptism at the hands of
John to teach in the synagogue at Nazareth and hear
him tell his fellow-townsmen such plain unpleasant truths

that they tried to throw him over the brow of the hill; when I listen to him shattering his fellow Israelites' complacent belief that they were the special favorites of God; when I watch him rebuke the fawning Pharisees even at the tables where they were entertaining him; when I hear him uttering things that hurt his own beloved disciples; I realize that Jesus was a teacher who did not hesitate to say what he believed, whatever it might cost. He was not one who said comfortable things to make people feel good or feared to disillusion his listeners with regard to their cherished errors. If, therefore, he had not shared the belief in immortality, he would have told his people. And it is to this fact he himself called attention when, on the last night of his life he looked with his disciples toward the life beyond the grave, and said, "If it were not so I would have told you." He was asking them to face the tomorrows on the basis of his own frankness in the yesterdays. "Ye believe in God; believe also in me."

The acid test of a man's belief in immortality is the confidence with which he confronts his own death. It is one thing to talk bravely about the hereafter; it is another thing to walk through the valley of the shadow of death and show no fear of evil. Jesus did not talk much about death. His was not the attitude of a man in the dark whistling to keep up his courage. He lived as if he took eternal life for granted. On the night before his crucifixion, the Fourth Gospel interprets him as saying, "Be of good cheer. I have overcome the world." Jesus walked to the brink of death, and then took the plunge into its depths as the graceful diver leaps from his high perch, trusting the buoyancy of the water into which he is dropping.

But, perhaps, although Jesus was honest in his belief, he too might have been mistaken? Well, we have had nineteen hundred years now to study the teachings of Jesus about this world which we can see. And if there is any one fact which grows more luminous as the centuries pass, it is that Jesus was right about the rules of living. Society grows more complex and artificial, but through the maze of human relationships the secret shines brighter that Jesus' principle of love is the only way by which men can dwell together in lasting amity. Business forms its billion dollar banks and individual incomes surpass the wealth of all first century Jerusalem —but amid the vastness of them, it grows ever clearer that the principles of service laid down by the penniless teacher of Palestine must predominate if the world of finance is to be saved. Nations still go to war, but in the seething cauldron of the great conflict is distilled the crystal conviction that Jesus' way of life is the only program for governments as well as for persons. The test of the ages tells us that Jesus was not mistaken about the world this side of the grave. If we have found him so utterly reliable in the life here which we can see, shall we not trust him in regard to the life which we have not seen, for be it remembered that in the teaching of Jesus the two hang together? Fundamental to all Jesus' gospel is the Fatherhood of God, and if God is a Father, immortality is inevitable. "If (we) being evil know how to give good gifts unto your children, how much more shall your Father which is in heaven give good things to them that ask him?" [2] It is unthinkable in fatherhood to deny this deepest desire of the heart.

Then, too, this Man of Nazareth has had a career since his crucifixion. I have some difficulty with the various reports of the Resurrection. But I have more difficulty in trying to explain the rise of Christianity without the triumph of Christ's personality over the tomb. Something happened which changed the crushed and dispirited disciples into radiant confident heralds of a triumphant Christ. Do you say the disciples were deceived by an illusion or a ghost story? But do ghost stories beget moral grandeur in those who believe them? Nobility and strength of character were the results of the Easter event. And what is more, those character results have been multiplying down the centuries. If you can believe that the Christian movement began by preaching a myth and has spread itself around the world by proclaiming a false hope, producing thereby such true characters as Francis of Assisi and Wilfred Grenfell, then you may dismiss Jesus of Nazareth as one more mistaken idealist lured to his death by a false dream. But for myself, I believe in the integrity of Jesus while he lived in the flesh and in the persistence of his personality after his crucifixion. And on the basis of his integrity I am disposed to trust his assumptions beyond the last frontier.

I cannot close this testimony without adding that I believe in a life beyond the grave because I trust the integrity of my own intimations of immortality.

[2] Matthew 7: 11.

The Master spoke of "inheriting eternal life." We enter into our inheritance of eternal life by gradual steps just as we enter into an earthly parental inheritance. A son may not take title to his father's property until after the parent's death, but he begins inheriting from his father through heredity in a prenatal state, and he goes on inheriting from his father through all the days of their fellowship together. Qualities, attitudes, tastes—these real properties of the soul pass from parent to child all along the way. So when we walk with our Heavenly Father by keeping spiritual comradeship with the highest revelation of him we know in the personality of Jesus, we find ourselves entering progressively into our inheritance of eternal life. Thus we work our way into an appreciation of immortal living as we work our way into an appreciation of immortal music or immortal art.

In short, I have lived long enough to know that when I live most like Christ, the eternal quality of life seems most natural and sure. In my worldly moods, death seems like a dispossess notice, removing me from all that makes life worth living. But as President Wishart of Wooster College has suggested, suppose that we were to go to Atlantic City and sit on the boardwalk watching the Easter parade of tourists. What a sense of transiency would sweep over us! The restlessly moving throng, the changing styles of dress, the midway shops with their offerings of momentary appeal—everything in the picture would suggest change and impermanence. But suppose we were to turn our backs on the holiday throng and look out to sea. What a different mood would be stirred in us by the movements of the waters on the great deep! They are restful in their restlessness, symbolic of illimitable reach and endless endurance.

Similarly Christ turns our backs on the passing show, the baubles of Vanity Fair, the changing worldliness, and directs our gaze out to the vast deeps of things unseen and eternal until we begin to get a sense of the boundlessness of life. We feel with Whittier both the infinitude and the intimacy of God, until we too say:

> I know not where his islands lift
> Their fronded palms in air;
> I only know I cannot drift
> Beyond his love and care.

In my experience this feeling of trust grows with growth. Life, as we have tried to show in these chapters, has a growing edge. Present any limit to its possibilities, and we immediately think beyond it. If, for instance, an insurance company could issue a policy that we should die not before, but on, our eightieth birthday, would we sign up? The chances are that most of us will not reach the four-score milestone, but we prefer to take the chance of passing it. We live in the domain of the more-yet-to-be. The more we learn, the more we feel remains to be learned. Even Isaac Newton, after all his scientific achievements, confessed: "I seem to have been like a boy playing on the seashore while the great ocean of truth lay all undiscovered before me." The larger the body of knowledge we survey, the longer the shoreline of mystery surrounding it. We crave the glory of going on because we have caught the tang of the sea that makes it possible.

And my furtive but growing intimations of eternal living are fortified by the confidence of those who have lived larger and better lives. Shortly before his death, one of the grand old men of American letters, Lyman Abbott, wrote: "I look forward to the Great Adventure, with awe but not with apprehension. I enjoy my work, my home, my friends, my life. I shall be very sorry to part with them. But always I have stood in the bow looking forward with hopeful anticipation to the life before me. When the time comes for my embarkation and the ropes are cast off and I put out to sea, I think I shall be standing in the bow and still looking forward with eager curiosity and glad hopefulness to the new world to which the unknown voyage will bring me."

Thus the good life passes the last frontier.

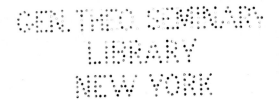

Pg. 27

Pg. 58